SEXUAL SUBORDINATION AND STATE INTERVENTION

Comparing Sweden and the United States

Sexual Subordination and State Intervention

Comparing Sweden and the United States

R. Amy Elman

Berghahn Books
Providence • Oxford

Published in 1996 by

Berghahn Books
Editorial offices:
165 Taber Avenue, Providence, RI 02906, USA
Bush House, Merewood Avenue, Oxford, OX3 8EF, UK

© 1996 R. Amy Elman
All rights reserved.
No part of this publication may be reproduced
in any form or by any means without the
written permission of Berghahn Books.

Library of Congress Cataloging-in-Publication Data
Elman, R. Amy, 1961–
   Sexual subordination and state intervention : comparing Sweden
and the United States / by R. Amy Elman
     p. cm.
   Includes bibliographical references (p.   ) and index.
   ISBN 1-57181-071-4 (hard : alk. paper). -- ISBN 1-57181-072-2
(pbk. : alk. paper)
   1. Abused women--Sweden. 2. Abused women--United States.
3. Abused women----Government policy--Sweden. 4. Abused
women--Government policy--United States.   I. Title.
HV6626.23.S8E44   1995   95-31518
362.82'928'09485--dc20   CIP

British Library Cataloguing in Publication Data
A CIP catalogue record for this book is available from
the British Library.

Printed in the United States on acid-free paper

CONTENTS

PREFACE	vii
ACKNOWLEDGMENTS	xii
ABBREVIATIONS	xiii

1. **THE ANALYTIC CONTEXT: GENDER-SPECIFICITY AND STATE STRUCTURES**   1
   The Structure of Each State 4
      Corporatist Sweden 4
      The Federalist United States 5
   State-Centered Analysis: Bringing Women in 7
      Gender-Neutrality: Women at Work and Within Families 7
      Gender-Specificity As a Conceptual Tool 11
   The Politics of Battery, Rape, and Sexual Harassment 13

2. **THE COMPARATIVE CONTEXT: STATE STRUCTURES, CULTURES, AND MOVEMENTS**   16
   Suffrage: The First Wave of Feminism 16
   The United States 20
      A Federalist Republic and Fragmented State 20
      American Political Culture 21
      American Feminism: Structural and Cultural Advantages 24
   Sweden 26
      A Centralized, Accommodating, and Expansive State 26
      Swedish Political Culture 28
      Swedish Feminism: Structural and Cultural Constraints 29
   Summary 31

3. **STATE INTERVENTION AND WOMAN BATTERY**   33
   The United States 35
      Autonomous Shelters 35
   Sweden 39
      State-Sanctioned Shelters 39
   The Criminal Justice Systems: Common Obstacles 43
      The American Case 44
      The Swedish Case 51
   Summary 59

4. STATE INTERVENTION AND RAPE 61
The United States 65
    Consciousness, Crisis Centers, and Other Support Services 65
Sweden 71
    Authoritative Discourse and Few Rape Crisis Services 71
The Criminal Justice Systems: Common Obstacles 77
    The American Case 79
    The Swedish Case 86
Summary 91

5. STATE INTERVENTION AND SEXUAL HARASSMENT 94
The United States 97
    The Discovery and Documentation of Sexual Harassment 97
    Legal Battles and Administrative Redress 99
Sweden 105
    The Identification of Sexual Harassment 105
    Legal Remedy Requested and Redress Deferred 110
Summary 112

6. CONCLUSION 115
Sweden 116
The United States 119
Closing Thoughts 121

REFERENCES 125

INDEX 140

Preface

Sweden, unlike most other states, is consistently portrayed as a highly advanced state that vigorously promotes women's well-being. This characterization is sustained by the presence of progressive labor and family-oriented policies and by scholars who presuppose that the development of social policies in such areas reveals a state's general concern for women and a commitment to sexual equality.[1] The relatively unimpressive reputation of the United States is similarly maintained. The assumption, then, is that the Swedish state is more responsive to women than the American state. This assumption is ill-conceived. We need to revise the very basis upon which we conduct comparative studies.

While states adopt policies on issues such as job training and daycare that may prove beneficial to women, such policies may result less from a commitment to gender equality than from a desire to efficiently meet the long-term interests of capital.[2] Because progressive policies for working women and mothers often stem from efforts to diminish labor shortages or foster children's welfare, they fail to provide a rigorous criterion for assessing a state's willingness or capacity to eradicate *gender* inequality. Until now, comparative studies have focused almost exclusively on progressive policies related to women and have avoided those that are gender-specific, for example, sexual abuse policies.

Ending women's oppression necessitates both a broader understanding of the state and the demand that the state mitigate oppressive conditions specific to women. I contend that an analysis of a

---

1. Social policy is broadly defined to mean state actions that affect the social status and life chances of individuals and groups.

2. Even abortion rights may be granted less because they are essential to women's bodily autonomy than because population planners wish to limit the population. Liberal men may also support abortion without a commitment to women's equality but with the expectation of increased sexual access to women. It is important to note that feminists in the United States initially desired the repeal of all abortion laws and were opposed to state regulation through legislation (Baehr 1990). For a brilliant analysis of how states have legalized abortion while isolating it from women's claims to bodily integrity, see Twiss Butler (1990).

state's response to battery, rape, and sexual harassment provides a better and more direct method of assessing its approach to gender equality, both because these abuses are central to maintaining women's subordination and because states lack an additional incentive for addressing them.[3] Consequently, a state's attempts to diminish woman abuse, or to punish the men who commit such abuse, reveals its responsiveness to women themselves.

This book is a comparative examination of how two differently structured states, Sweden and the United States, have responded to the physical and sexual assault of women. While it explores feminist efforts to politicize such abuse, the primary focus is on the development and implementation of specific public policies and programs designed to provide women relief from the men who abuse them.[4]

It does not offer a comparative analysis of the scope of battery, rape, and sexual harassment, as data regarding these abuses are often unreliable; statistics are relatively recent or absent, and these crimes are notoriously underreported. Moreover, fewer reported incidents in one state may reflect less the exceptionality of their occurrence than their pervasiveness. To report a crime one must not only perceive oneself to have been victimized but must also believe that reporting the crime will offer some relief. A higher level of reporting may, therefore, indicate a greater belief in the state's capacity to rectify sexual oppression. It may also indicate a greater awareness among women to consider that their abuse is criminal. On the other hand, a higher level of reporting may reflect a higher level of abuse.

Precisely because such statistics can be interpreted so differently, they do not offer a reliable picture of the scope of battery, rape, and sexual harassment. Although cross-national research cannot indicate with certainty whether the level of sexual abuse and violence

---

3. Some may insist, however, that states do have incentives to end these abuses. For example, one could argue that when the American state acts against these harms it protects itself from the costs of litigation. While this is true, the American state does not necessarily benefit from this action. Instead, American feminists have effectively discouraged state apathy. That is, in the United States feminists have been able to force the state's hand to mitigate gender-specific harm. They have utilized lawsuits and other strategies to this end. See Chapters 3–5.

4. Throughout this work, the term "feminist" is broadly employed to refer to women actively involved to end male dominance, brutality, and sexual abuse. To speak of feminism in an unmodified manner—without the additional labels of "socialist," "radical," "liberal," or "lesbian"—is to focus primarily on the political commitment of women to women, as women. Such woman-identification distinguishes feminism from other movements and ideologies (MacKinnon 1987).

against women is higher in Sweden or in the United States, it can, in general terms, reveal the capacities of both states to recognize and respond to these abuses when they do appear.

I formally began the research for this book in 1988 with a series of twenty open-ended interviews with Swedish bureaucrats, feminist activists, party members, criminal justice personnel, battered women's shelter workers, and the founders of what was once Sweden's only rape crisis clinic.[5] These initial interviews, which ranged from one to two hours, helped to establish the parameters of my case studies. I was to learn that Sweden had only recently adopted a handful of reforms relating to violence against women (dating from 1986) and that it had just commissioned an investigation of sexual harassment but had yet to adopt any specific countermeasures. A majority of these interviews continued as informal conversations, and I was provided with unpublished manuscripts and numerous additional contacts.

In exploring women's sexual subordination, my methodology is grounded in feminism and what social scientists have regarded as "participant observation."[6] Participant observation is a firmly established, systematic approach to social science research that entails participation in the "daily life" of those one studies. It is premised in the appreciation that one's understanding of others is enhanced when one is prepared to invest himself or herself in a relationship (Oakley 1981, 41). Consequently, formal interviews often evolve into ongoing conversations and an active involvement in the community one studies. R. Emerson Dobash and Russell Dobash have utilized this method. In their work *Women, Violence and Social Change*, they explicitly refer to themselves as "activist researchers" (1992, viii). Other works have employed this same approach (Barry 1979; Bart and O'Brien 1985; Oakley 1981). For this study I became both an active participant in and observer of feminist politics in each country. This work is the result of seven years of numerous in-depth, open-ended interviews and conversations with public officials, feminist activists, and women harmed by rape, battery, or sexual harassment. Given the abundance of American scholarship and the dearth of Swedish secondary literature on these issues, I

---

5. The Swedish Institute originally facilitated my contact with those involved in the development and/or implementation of reforms for raped, battered, and sexually harassed women. Individuals whom I have cited within the text have been formally cited in the reference list.

6. For a feminist analysis of methodology, see Liz Stanley and Sue Wise's *Breaking Out Again: Feminist Ontology and Epistemology* (1993).

depended more heavily on primary sources (i.e., newspaper articles and interviews) for the Swedish half of this work. Indeed, a survey of eighty-two battered women in shelters throughout Sweden (Elman and Eduards 1991)—a survey that resulted from my work with Swedish feminists—was the first of its kind in that country. The findings of this survey are presented throughout the present volume. A myriad of other surveys, court cases, crime surveys, and various government documents from both countries are also provided throughout.

What follows is an analysis of each state's response to battered, raped, and sexually harassed women. In this work, I do not claim to capture the full diversity of women's experiences; nor do I insist that all women have been battered, raped, and/or sexually harassed. Rather, I wish to illuminate the manner in which such abuse affects women as a group and to provide a cross-national examination of the relation women have to their respective states and of the possibilities for social change.

This book results from my desire for sexual equality and therefore an end to the psychological terror and physical abuse directed specifically against women. The choice of these particular countries is the consequence of my familiarity with the United States and my constant search for an appealing alternative. Like so many, I turned to Sweden. To my surprise, after two years of living there, I realized that my familiarity with the weaknesses of my native country had hindered my appreciation of its relative strengths.

The Organization of the Text

The following chapters provide policy cases designed to illustrate, extend, and refine the argument that an examination of feminist attempts to use state mechanisms for social change specifically beneficial to women reveals the fragility of conventional characterizations of states and the opportunities for equality those states provide. This work is intentionally written within a comparative context. As a result, the particular dimensions of each state are best understood through comparison rather than through separate analyses. The assessments contained in this work are relational; Sweden is explored by contrast to the United States, and vice versa.

The first chapter summarizes the approach used to study state structure and women's issues cross-nationally. Chapter 2 offers a historical preface and cultural context within which to account for the structure of each state and its influence on the development of political movements which, in turn, shape policies pertaining to women. In particular, I argue that the American federalist state is conducive to an autonomous feminist movement while Sweden's centralized corporatist state is not because Swedish feminists are integrated into the traditional political system. Swedish women, as women, thus lack the political cohesion from which their American counterparts benefit in their fight against women's sexual subordination.

Subsequent chapters examine the different effects of autonomy and integration on feminist consciousness and the emergence and development of gender-specific policies and programs. A comparative survey of battery (Chapter 3) and rape (Chapter 4) reforms indicates that the Swedish state is less responsive than the American state to women's claims for relief. In Sweden, legislative and administrative reforms and programs are fewer and less comprehensive and were adopted later than in the United States. Moreover, the implementation of Swedish reforms is somewhat less impressive than in the United States, where authorities may be legally liable (i.e., financially responsible) for the ill enforcement of public policies.

The last case study concerns workplace sexual harassment. Given that such harassment is a form of sexual abuse and is perpetrated primarily by men against women workers, this chapter (Chapter 5) provides an excellent opportunity to assess a condition that affects women as workers. Despite its more direct relation to labor, this aspect of women's subordination again reveals that the Swedish state is less responsive to oppressive conditions specific to women. While the American state formally recognizes the existence of sexual harassment and has taken steps against it, the Swedish state has been slow to provide any legal remedy. Instead, Sweden's centralized state uses its organizational capacity to effectively cast the issue in terms that de-emphasize the gendered aspect of the abuse.

The conclusion (Chapter 6) provides a brief summary of my findings. It integrates my argument concerning the state's response to gender-specific claims with some general observations regarding the relationship of women to each state and the possibilities available to them for social change.

ACKNOWLEDGMENTS

I began this project in 1987. The financial support provided me by a Fulbright doctoral dissertation grant, the Dean's Office of New York University, and the Center for European Studies at Kalamazoo College helped me to complete this study. My sincere appreciation extends to Maud Landby Eduards, Lawrence Mead, Ted Perlmutter, Martin Schain, and Richard Sennett. They helped me begin this project; Martin Schain made certain that I would finish it.

I must also thank Bentley Fane, Peter Corrigan, Ralph Hummel, Cathy Potter, and Jean Robinson for reading this manuscript in various stages and helping me to improve upon it. Two colleagues from Kalamazoo College, Marigene Arnold and Gail Griffin, not only offered substantive criticisms on this manuscript but are to be credited with furthering feminism within the college.

My greatest debt, however, rests with the women whose activism, genius, and general support has been central to the development of this work. They are those who remain actively engaged in ending women's oppression in the United States and Sweden. These include Bettan Andersson, Pauline Bart, Kathleen Barry, Gerda Christensson, Karen Davis, Gun Englund, Eve Goodman, Donna Hughes, Ebon Kram, Dorchen Leidholdt, Maura Maguire, Renee Mittler, Florence Rush, Betsy Salkind, Agneta Sandell, Jane Welborn, Betsy Warrior, and Agneta Åkesson.

Lastly, I wish to acknowledge two close friends, Annie McCombs and Katinka Ström. Both provided essential research assistance and innumerable feminist insights. Without their help and friendship throughout the years, this book would not have been possible.

ABBREVIATIONS

BRÅ	Brottsförebyggande rådet (Sweden's National Council for Crime Prevention)
CDBG	Community Development Block Grant
CETA	Comprehensive Employment Training Act
Ds	Departementsserien (Series of reports published by Swedish Ministries)
EEOC	Equal Employment Opportunities Commission
JÄMO	Jämställdhetsombudsmannen (Sweden's Equality Ombudsman)
LEAA	Law Enforcement Assistance Administration
MSPB	Merit Systems Protection Board
NCADV	National Coalition Against Domestic Violence
NOW	National Organization for Women
NYRF	New York Radical Feminists
NYWAR	New York Women Against Rape
ODV	Office of Domestic Violence
RFSU	Riksförbundet för sexuell upplysning (Sweden's National Association for Sex Education)
ROKS	Riksorganisationen för kvinnojourer i Sverige (The National Organization of Emergency Shelters for Battered Women in Sweden)
SFS	Svensk författningssamling (Sweden's official publication of statutes)
SOU	Statens offentliga utredningar (Sweden's official investigatory reports)
VAWA	Violence Against Women Act
WOAR	Women Organized Against Rape
WWU	Working Women United

The Analytic Context
Gender-Specificity and State Structures

Scholars of the state have been reluctant to note that one of the most distinctive characteristics of any state is its gendered designation of legitimized force[1]—that states provide men, not women, with what Max Weber refers to as a "community that successfully claims the monopoly of the legitimate use of physical force within a given territory" (1981, 78).[2] Virginia Woolf notes this when she accounts for women's relative powerlessness within the state. She writes, "Our class is the weakest of all classes in the state. We have no weapons with which to enforce our will" (1966, 13). While Woolf is no scholar of the state, nonetheless, it is true that virtually every avenue of power within the state remains almost entirely under male control.

Although Sweden and the United States are, in this sense, "patriarchal" states,[3] discussions concerning their power have typically focused on characteristics other than gender. For example, one

---

1. Even the literature pertaining specifically to women and the state focuses instead on women as increasingly dependent on the state, as both employees and clients. See, for example, Elizabeth Wilson's *Women and the Welfare State* (1977), the numerous essays within Anne Showstack Sassoon's *Women and the State* (1987) and Linda Gordon's *Women, the State and Welfare* (1990). More recently, Drude Dahlerup takes a similar position in her essay, "Learning to Live With The State" in *Women's Studies International Forum* (1994). By contrast, Sylvia Walby argues that women's earlier "exclusion from the state has been replaced" not by their dependence on it but "by their subordination within it" (1990, 179). If one considers the centrality of the state to the maintenance of male power, one realizes that men benefit more from the state and, thus, may be more dependent on it than women.
2. States are more than mere governments; they consist of numerous systems and elusive methods of legal coercion that structure the relationships between civil society and public authority (Mitchell 1991, 1992; Stepan 1978; Weber 1981, 82).
3. The problem with the term "patriarchy" involves its literal meaning as "rule of the father." As Carole Pateman has argued, the ideological justifications for father-right were decisively defeated in seventeenth century debates throughout Europe. Pateman concludes: "the father is politically dead and his patriarchal power has been universalized, that is, distributed to all men ..." (1988a, 113).

or both of these states have been depicted as capitalist, socialist, imperialist, centralized, and decentralized. Like all modern states, Sweden and the United States have some of these attributes. Yet, regardless of their varied structures, cultures, or economic agendas, both states are fundamentally male-dominated. That is, men possess greater influence in establishing the parameters of political discourse and public policy. This fact has rarely received the critical scrutiny it merits.

A full theoretical account of the state and its connection to, and autonomy from, male dominance is a colossal task. It is made especially difficult because the "State and masculine domination both work through ... ubiquitousness rather than through tight, coherent strategies" (Brown 1992, 15). Yet, an analysis of the state's role in legitimizing and/or mitigating the most tangible expressions of male power provides an important beginning in accounting for state power.

This book begins to fill a void in state-centered research by examining how Sweden and the United States respond to women's sexual oppression. In particular, the focus will be on laws, policies, and programs concerning rape, battery, and sexual harassment. This work seeks to evaluate the commitment of these two very differently structured states to the mitigation of such sexual inequality while providing new insights into the ways states use power in general.

Scholars who study the state have frequently noted how states vociferously defend their territories from external threats and internal disorder (Skocpol 1985; Tilly 1992). However, they have ignored the state's role in encouraging or mitigating the violence and sexualized force male citizens direct against females. There is, however, an explanation for this oversight. The state itself has been constituted within a culturally defined public realm that has historically rebuffed intervention in those matters which have traditionally been conceived of as private, such as the physical and sexual abuse of women.

It would be naive to assume, however, that the historical reluctance of states to intervene in such "private matters" is capricious. After all, states monopolize the legitimate use of force only if they exercise restraint. Through the process of defining public policy, states thus ignore, tolerate, and even encourage particular expressions of force and violence, while discouraging others. In this manner, states decisively counter the threat of anarchy. Focusing on how, when, and against whom "legitimate" force is used provides a basic understanding of both the state and the civil relationships it helps to structure (Dobash 1990; Dobash and Dobash 1992). The apparent invisibility of the coercion that men use to secure their domination over women stems from our being unaccustomed to associating gender with conflict. Moreover, male domination is so thoroughly and universally accepted that "it scarcely seems to require violent implementation" (Millet 1970, 43). Nonetheless, many relationships between men and women are deeply rooted in force, if not violence, a truth only recently assessed as political through feminist texts.[4] And, within the last two decades, feminists in the United States and Sweden have challenged the public's indifference to sexual oppression; both states have begun to intervene and hence have become sites of conflict.

When states intervene to assuage the physical and sexual abuse of women, they can, in effect, delegitimize male force and violence against women. State intervention, therefore, has the *potential* to radically alter some of the most concrete expressions of gender inequality. The question is: Which state (structure) is most conducive to achieving the kind of intervention that can redress women's sexual subordination?

The fact that Sweden and the United States are pursuing many of the same goals to mitigate sexual inequality does not mean that they will do so in the same ways or that the outcomes will be similar. In each state, policies pertaining to battery, rape and sexual harassment are greatly influenced by the structure from which such policies and programs emerge and develop. The structures of these states differentially affect the access to authority, political consciousness, strategies, and cohesiveness of various interests (Esping-Anderson, Friedland, and Wright 1976).

The United States and Sweden are ideal subjects for a cross-national, state-centered investigation. Both are advanced industrial societies that have explicitly declared their commitment to gender equality and have organized political interest groups committed to ending sexual abuse and violence against women. They differ primarily in structure. This allows us to trace differences in their women's movements and resultant social policies to essential structural contrasts.

---

4. The fact that this had not, until recently, been a topic of research or reform does not imply an earlier absence of these abuses against women. Pleck (1987) has documented the severe abuse women sustained in the United States since the colonial period. Dahlberg (1989) has provided similar information about Sweden.

The Structure of Each State

Corporatist Sweden

Sweden is a corporatist state, insofar as public policy results from a highly institutionalized form of group access. The corporatist state is neither an "arena for which interests contend" nor "another interest group with which they compete, but a constitutive element engaged in defining, distorting, encouraging, regulating, licensing and/or repressing the activities of associations" (Schmitter 1982, 260). Political and economic power is so centralized that the state is able to successfully depoliticize certain issues while defining the terms of political participation for others.

Until recently, the division of resources, services, and benefits was largely the product of tripartite agreements—between government officials, employers, and organized labor—at the national level.[5] The last conservative government (1991–1994) together with a recalcitrant employer's confederation and weakened labor obviate the tripartite character of this state. This does not, however, mean that Sweden is no longer a corporatist state. After all, states retain their character long after governments attempt to alter them.

Swedish policy-making power is still concentrated in the Prime Minister's cabinet, where ministers hold primary power and responsibility for policy formulation. The cabinet often represents the party (or coalition) that controls a majority of the seats within the Riksdag (i.e., Sweden's parliament) and reflects its policies.

Yet Swedish policy also reflects the preferences of opposition parties and interest groups. Through formal, extensive consultation procedures that precede the preparation of policy, the state's ministries selectively call upon a limited number of interest groups for their suggestions and opinions (Kelman 1981). Additionally, the cabinet or appropriate ministry appoints commissions to study and suggest reforms to address those policy issues that they consider to be important. Typically, such commissions include representatives from each party, state bureaucrats, appropriate interest groups, and experts. Through the involvement of all these political actors in policy-making, the corporatist state achieves social cohesion and integration (Heclo and Madsen 1987) and thus ensures the cooperation of numerous sectors in the implementation of policy.

---

5. And, since local administrators work within national guidelines, Hernes and Selvik suggest that corporatism even reproduces itself on the local level (1981).

The very inclusiveness that encourages successful policy implementation may, however, hinder bold attempts at reform. Corporatism encourages a process through which selected interest groups engage in political exchange and are held clearly responsible for outcomes. The policy process may have conservatizing consequences; groups may avoid radical departures for which they would be accountable. A more dispersed polity in which groups need be less responsible may be able to consider a wider range of options— including those that are specifically feminist.

The desire to obtain state funding and participate in policy decisions may, in addition, serve as a restraint on a group's or individual's activities.[6] In Sweden, nonprofit organizations are not autonomous from the state. Organizations must, therefore, compromise more radical agendas because they rely so heavily on state funding. An interest group's ability to claim representational monopoly depends on its obtaining the state's favor, and from this favor comes official state recognition, resources, and access to policy-making. The ambition to be incorporated by the state, or officially recognized by it, may restrain interest groups' criticism of government policies. This situation frequently renders those interested in fundamental transformation vulnerable, invisible, and silent.

The result of such state-society relations is clear: leadership emerges from those who often have more in common with each other than with their constituents. Consequently, the corporatist state ensures its power base and the status quo remains essentially unaltered. In Sweden, criticisms are modified, conflicts are avoided, and protests are infrequent (Gelb 1987; Heclo and Madsen 1987).

The Federalist United States

Compared to Sweden's structure, the structure of the American state is radically dispersed. Within the United States, political parties are relatively nonprogrammatic and the realms of bureaucratic administration are fragmented. Scholars assert that the fragmentation of authority has consistently discouraged a unified and persistent class politics, encouraged divisions within capital, and undermined national welfare initiatives (Weir, Orloff, and Skocpol 1988). Additionally, federalism encourages differences between regions and communities to develop.

---

6. No individual or organization is going to bite the hand that feeds it. This will be further discussed as the book proceeds. See especially Chapter 3 for a comparative analysis of funding for battered women's shelters in Sweden and the United States.

Within this loosely structured state, interest groups enjoy more autonomy from the state than their Swedish counterparts, in the sense that they are not exclusively reliant on the state for funding or political support. They have many more avenues, within the state, through which they can pursue their own agendas. Relative to the Swedish state, the American state accords greater access to groups that wish to participate in politics and have acquired the resources to do so. The structure of the federalist state lacks the institutional means to regulate interest groups. Consequently, American interest groups compete with one another for their share of political and economic power in determining public policy.

The implementation of national policies becomes difficult, because national leaders must rely on state and local governments to enforce these policies. Furthermore, the implementation of public policy is notoriously difficult because each loosely structured governing coalition at the federal or local level faces constant pressures from opposing interests (Lowi 1979). If federalism inhibits the implementation of broad (national) reforms, however, interest groups may also enjoy great political access through which they can assert a wide range of innovative claims.

In federalist states, like the United States, there is a high level of political activity at the local level and a greater demarcation between national and local level policy concerns than in Sweden. Therefore, issues dismissed and/or delegated as non-national interests are decided by state and local governments. Significantly, it is at the local level that most of the policies which specifically affect women emerge and are implemented.

The American state has consistently been portrayed as "weak" because of its late bureaucratization, its decentralized structure, and, especially, its reluctance to mitigate class inequities. All interests, however, do not have the same potential for effective political organizing. While some interests become central, others are excluded. Although the structural fragmentation of the United States may have compromised its capacity to develop extensive welfare initiatives, decentralization has not necessarily had the same effect on other issues. In particular, while the corporatist structure of the Swedish state may be more responsive to gender-neutral, labor-related claims, the federalist United States may be more responsive to claims specific to women.

Steven Krasner reminds us that "states may be strong in some issue areas and weak in others" (1978, 58). He spurns *a priori* assumptions concerning states and their capacities. Additionally, Diane Sainsbury writes: "Theories of women and politics—both of a descriptive and normative nature—have produced generalizations divorced from a consideration of variations of country-specific contexts" (1988, 344). This study proceeds from such caution and insight.

Given the current research on these two states, one would expect that the American state would be more permeable to women's demands but less capable of, and more resistant to, enforcing reforms specifically beneficial to women. By comparison, the Swedish state would be less accessible to women's demands but more effective in implementing policies for women. This book challenges this conventional assessment.

State-Centered Analysis: Bringing Women in

Gender-Neutrality: Women at Work and Within Families

Most comparative analyses of Sweden and the United States exclude a consideration of those conflicts that are essentially gendered. This is the case even in literature that explicitly pertains to women. Comparative political studies on the contemporary subordination of women focus almost exclusively on women's position in the wage labor market and/or family.[7] Consequently, women are analytically reduced to "workers" and/or mothers; consideration of women's lives outside of these two roles is conspicuously absent.

Having focused, without exception, on this particular aspect of women's lives, comparativists of Sweden and the United States share a common judgment: Sweden is better for women. Scholars note that, relative to their American counterparts, Swedish women have greater access to childcare, worker benefits, and job-training programs and enjoy a greater presence in the labor market. These scholars, however, attribute this finding to a host of different factors: the party system, leftist parties, organized labor, state ideology, state structure, or a combination of these elements. Although Carolyn

---

7. While the literature reviewed in this work is specifically concerned with Sweden and/or the United States, I believe that this characterization could hold for comparative literature relating to other countries as well.

One exception is Joyce Gelb's comparative study of Great Britain and the United States which contains a brief look at Sweden (1990). Although her primary focus is labor-related issues, she does provide a cursory overview of "domestic violence" and rape. Yet, the fact that this discussion is brief and entitled "Other women's related issues" (Gelb 1990, 171) suggests that, like other comparativists, she has failed to distinguish the characteristics of gender-specific issues from others related to women. This will be discussed in greater depth as the chapter proceeds.

Teich Adams and Kathryn Teich Winston (1980) emphasize the interventionist ideology of governments in regard to the family,[8] they share with Mary Ruggie (1984) the thesis that progressive policies for women stem from Sweden's centralized state. Ruggie also credits labor for placing women's interests on the public agenda, and Pippa Norris (1987) credits leftist parties. Others (Verba, et al., 1987) assert that feminists have their issues resolved through Sweden's strong party system itself.

Scholars differ in their emphases, yet all openly acknowledge the absence of an autonomous feminist movement through which women in Sweden could otherwise press their claims (Adams and Winston 1980; Gelb 1987; Norris 1987; Ruggie 1984; Scott 1982).[9] Far from being perceived as a liability for Swedish women, non-Swedish scholars have refused to mourn the absence of an autonomous feminist movement. Norris, in fact, considers the absence of such a movement to be a positive sign for women. She believes that societies with "low-profile" feminist movements more willingly accept feminist demands. This explanation accounts for her findings that while American women are conscious of sexual inequality and well-organized in representing their interests, there is a "marked contradiction between conscious expectations and objective political and social conditions" (1987, 144). Furthermore, she argues that, despite the absence of a militant feminist movement in Sweden, women there have progressed further toward equality than have women in the United States.

8. Adams and Winston suggest that Swedish "government agencies have the right, even the obligation, to intervene in families in order to protect the community's interest in the family" (1980, 253). Yet, having analytically transmuted "woman" into "the family," they say nothing of governmental intervention to promote a woman's individual well-being. Instead, they write, "In Sweden, this intervention is confined to matters involving child welfare" (1980, 253).

9. The term movement refers to a network of grass-roots organizations that seeks to alter public opinion and policy. To insist on the relative absence of an autonomous Swedish feminist movement is not to deny the existence of numerous individual feminists, their particular actions/events, nor the few feminist spaces that do exist. This is simply to acknowledge the lack of an extensive feminist network and protest movement.

Within Sweden, it is far more common to find women's liberationists, as opposed to feminists. Although the former are interested in equality between women and men, they are often engaged in progressive networks that are not specifically engaged in fighting against women's oppression. Confusion, however, persists. The Social Democratic women's section, while in opposition, called for the word "feminist" to be used in the party platform in time for the 1994 election (*The European*, 12–15 August 1993, 14).

The Swedish political system, however, did not formulate programs to support working women as a response to an overwhelming constituency demand from women themselves (Adams and Winston 1980, 137–138). In other words, Sweden's progressive labor and daycare policies cannot be seen as concessions to feminists. It is ironic that in the absence of a strong women's movement this literature does not conclude that the interests of women have been compromised. But, as discussed below, women in both the United States and Sweden are not the primary beneficiaries of the progressive politics of daycare and other work-related policies that encourage their entrance into the labor market.

In both countries, state policies concerning abortion, family planning, and childcare, along with progressive worker policies, all of which can benefit women, may exhibit a greater commitment to capital and/or welfare in general than to women specifically. These policies are not necessarily a measure through which one can assess the state's responsiveness to the particular needs of women as women. States may institute these policies simply as one way to mobilize women in the labor force as workers. One cannot assume that policy makers provide women employment opportunities to promote sexual equality.[10] After all, male dominance within the wage labor market has not significantly diminished with women's presence. In fact, Mary Ruggie asserts that women in Sweden entered the work force because of "the robust economic growth Sweden was experiencing" and not because men desired gender equality (1984, 162). Christina Jonung and Bodil Thordarsson's thesis is somewhat more critical (1980). They attribute women's entrance into the labor market to a labor shortage and the fact that, after the mid-1960s, Swedish unions viewed women as a preferable alternative to the continued use of immigrant labor. Jennifer Schirmer perceptively notes that Scandinavian corporatist welfare states develop progressive employment and childcare policies to meet the needs of capital and not necessarily the needs of women (1982).

While Lisa Leghorn and Katherine Parker also acknowledge the benefits capital derives from progressive policies, they insist that men, in particular, profit from them. They write:

---

10. Similarly, Carole Pateman notes that the continuing "perception of democracy as a class problem and the influence of liberal feminists have combined to keep alive Engel's old solution to 'the woman question'—to bring the whole female sex back into public industry" (1988b, 258).

women's "equality" means a more efficient use of human capital, more incomes to tax, more skilled labor to fill their labor shortage, and greater support for their party from women ... men's status is not diminished. When men are deciding the path to equality, it is designed for their purposes. (1981, 78–79)

These authors, furthermore, claim that Sweden's progressive policies even encourage the patriarchal family to remain the basic social unit. They support this assertion by showing that the most generous support for women has gone to mothers.

Although policies designed to provide women with childcare, financial support, and/or diverse employment opportunities are an essential condition for achieving an egalitarian state, they do not necessarily demonstrate a state's responsiveness to the needs of women *as* women. In fact, some Swedish women have objected to the way the male labor movement and political leaders use the guises of "equality" and "family policy" to discuss women (Gelb 1987; Hirdman 1994).

American feminist researchers express similar frustrations. When considering American social policies, Virginia Sapiro confirms the findings of Leghorn and Parker. She writes, "Most social policy aimed at women has been designed explicitly to benefit them in their capacity as wives and mothers and, more particularly, to benefit those who depend most upon them for nurturance and domestic service" (1986, 230). Thus, she argues that American women have been the main conduits of policies developed to meet the needs of others, in particular children.[11] Similarly, Swedish women have historically been the main conduits of policies developed to diminish labor shortages. Such policies may actually benefit women, but they are not a reliable index of the state's response to them.

Since there is little that is distinctively woman-specific about these policies, they can provide only a partial indicator of the state's autonomy from male interests and its responsiveness to the concerns of women as women. Because women are a social group that is often defined and exploited through means largely independent of the organization of material production, it is vital that an analysis of the state with regard to women appreciate that "economically conditioned power is not identical with power as such."[12] Indeed, as Weber

---

11. She cites as her examples the widow's pensions, the Sheppard-Towner Act, and AFDC.

12. While undoubtedly one could argue that economically independent women are likely to be freer from sexual coercion and violence, two points need to be considered. First, it is a fact that women of all socioeconomic classes are subjected to sexual abuse

has so aptly stated, "the emergence of economic power may be the consequence of power existing on other grounds" (1981, 180).

Gender-Specificity As a Conceptual Tool

Gender as a determinant of power rarely receives the scholarly attention it deserves. Approaches that have sought to analyze the inextricability of race, class, and gender have frequently subsumed gender-related issues while claiming to do otherwise. As Kimberlè Williams Crenshaw writes, "traditional readings of racism continue to center on power differences between men" (1992, 419).[13] Similarly, in works that attempt to address the inextricable character of patriarchy and capitalism, "economic causality takes precedence" (Scott 1988, 35). Male dominance, thus, remains intact and male concerns are privileged. More specifically, the study of family policies and occupational opportunities, however sophisticated, cannot reveal how a state responds to the particular needs of women. Such policies are not reliable as indicators of women's power because they are designed to affect workers and families, not women specifically. Only a "gender-specific"[14] issue can provide a reliable picture of a state's responsiveness to the needs of women, as women.

---

and male violence. Secondly, a relative lack of financial resources is not the only factor that infringes on women's ability to escape abusive men. This will be further discussed in Chapter 3, which deals specifically with battered women.

13. To best address the "interplay of gender and race in cultural and political discourse on violence," Crenshaw proposes an "intersectional framework" (Crenshaw 1993, 112). This approach focuses on those "sites where race and gender converge to create the cultural and political grounding for gender violence" (Crenshaw 1993, 113). While the utility of this approach is unquestionably beneficial for an analysis of the United States or any other single state study, there are important and justifiable reasons that this cross-national investigation places a greater emphasis on gender as a category of analysis. Stated simply, comparison involves comparability.

For Europeans the historical and analytical dimensions pertaining to race and racism are markedly different. "Race," within a European context, has historically denoted various ethnic groups. With the rise of Nazism and the growing influence of Nazi terminology, "race" was a term used to denote the supposed genetic differences among European groups, including Jews, all of whom were white. Only after World War II did those in the United States come to use "race" in a relatively more anthropological sense to refer, above all, to differences between whites and blacks. Nonetheless, important distinctions persist between the social meanings that Europeans and North Americans attach to "race." Thus, while race could perhaps be a comparative category of analysis in, for example, an exploration of immigration in Sweden, the analytical bearing of such comparisons would be unclear, if not tokenistic, for this cross-national study of sexual oppression.

14. It has commonly been understood that the distinction between gender and sex is that the former is socially constructed and the latter is biologically determined. Even

The sexual abuse and battery of women is *gender-specific* because not only does it *happen to women* (as women), regardless of their class position, race, or ethnicity, but it is *perpetrated predominantly by men* regardless of their class, race, or ethnicity (Martin 1976; Russell 1984). Indeed, with the exception of gender, there are no known characteristics that distinguish rapists and batterers from nonrapists and nonbatterers. What is known is that women are most frequently harmed, in a private context, by the men who are supposedly closest to them.

Feminism, with its gender-specific perspective, seeks to "extract the truth of women's commonalities out of the lie that all women are the same" (MacKinnon 1983, 639). While not all women are or have been raped and/or battered, feminists have recognized that the fear of rape and violence against women permeates all women's lives (Rich 1979). Although some men, as Marilyn Frye suggests, may exhibit concern over the sexual and physical abuse of women, they have a different reaction and relationship to it than women. Men may become outraged when a woman has been beaten or raped by another man. Yet, while some men view this male behavior contemptuously, Frye notes the possibility that their contempt is not premised in the occurrence of the abuse, but rather from the batterer or rapist choosing to accomplish by force what they, themselves, can achieve more subtly—power over women (1983, 72).

Feminism uniquely exposes rape and battery as terrorist acts within a systematic context of group subjection as opposed to isolated incidents or moral transgressions. Because politics refers to "power-structured relationships—arrangements whereby one group is controlled by another" (Millett 1970, 23), feminists consider rape and woman battery to be political acts, each a gendered technique of control utilized to enforce women's subordination. Though essentially uninterested in the gendered aspects of coercion, Charles Tilly understands that "coercion works." He writes, "those who apply substantial force to their fellows [sic] get compliance, and from that compliance draw multiple advantages of money, goods, deference, access to pleasures denied to less powerful people" (1992, 70).

---

with this distinction, however, the relation of sexuality to both remains obscure. Yet, like Catharine A. MacKinnon, I believe that biology provides social meaning to sexuality within patriarchy and that "sexuality is fundamental to gender and [is] fundamentally social" (1983, 635). Therefore, like MacKinnon, I will use the terms sex and gender interchangeably with reference to sexuality.

Sexual abuse and battery of women, more than any other oppressive circumstance, readily demonstrate the presence of gender conflict, coercion, and inequality. State policy regarding sexual abuse and woman battering, therefore, constitutes a more accurate measure of a state's autonomy from or complicity with male power as well as its responsiveness to women as a group. This is so precisely because the state appears to have little other (i.e., economic or social) incentive for redressing this kind of inequality.[15]

The Politics of Battery, Rape, and Sexual Harassment

In the past, discussions of male brutality and sexual abuse were kept so private that public solutions and state intervention were considered inappropriate. Most people have been more inclined to deny or ignore women's gender-specific oppression than to change it. Therefore, the fact that battery, rape, and sexual harassment had not, until recently, been topics of research or reform does not imply an earlier absence of abuses against women.[16] These issues were simply deemed both academically and politically irrelevant. Few people were ready to challenge the privacy of "family life" or "personal relations" and the authority of men within them. Emphasizing privacy, moreover, precludes the recognition that rape and woman battery are prevalent and diminishes the importance of these abuses as social problems and political issues.

Women's sexual oppression is not, however, something that occurs only within a domestic context. Sexual harassment in the workplace is the public expression of women's sexualized subordination. It essentially undermines the integrity and control that women ought to have over their bodies. But, unlike other forms of sexual subordination, workplace sexual harassment more directly involves the "reciprocal enforcement of two inequalities: the sexual and economic." While a woman's sexuality is used to coerce her economically, her position of employment is used to coerce her sexually (MacKinnon 1979, 7).

15. Some insist that, were the state aware of the serious effects of sexual abuse and violence against women on women's productivity, the prevention of these crimes would constitute a greater component of state policy. However, these crimes are primarily an expression of male power, and states are designed to protect and reinforce the (male) social order. Consequently, states are also dissuaded from intervening on women's behalf (Ferraro 1994).

16. See note 4 above and 17 below.

Feminists in the United States and Sweden have challenged the public's tolerance of sexual harassment, rape, and woman battery.[17] The reemergence of violence against women and of sexual abuse as issues of public concern occurred in the United States in the early 1970s when matters regarding social responsibility and equality dominated public discourse. A similar concern was expressed in Sweden nearly a decade later.[18] Women in both states began to evaluate their personal experiences of sexual subordination in political terms. Their discussion of sexual harassment in the workplace revealed the sexual dimensions of employment discrimination and occupational segregation. And, in both countries, rape and battery came to exemplify the horror and brutality involved in women's oppression. As a consequence of the awareness feminists promoted, action became necessary.

Women began to assert that, as citizens, they were entitled to protection from the men who harassed and terrorized them. Thus, it is hardly surprising that women working to end sexual abuse and battery and provide women relief came to rely on the state for social assistance and on the law as an instrument of reform.

As a result of their efforts, state actors increasingly intervened in both the United States and Sweden. Legislative reforms were instituted, through which penalties and various other restraints were imposed on men, and social programs and services were established to provide women relief. Perhaps these reforms were enacted, in part, to legitimize the state and rationalize the contradiction of women's compromised safety and status within countries that promised equality.

To fully account for the determinants of reform is an impossible task. Yet reformers assert that, despite its "patriarchal aspect," states have the potential to provide women relief from the men who abuse them (Elman 1989; MacKinnon 1989). This belief is what inspires their movements to seek redress through the state.

Some tend to describe reforms as concessions from those who have power (Piven and Cloward 1971, 1977; Wilson 1977), while others insist they are thinly disguised adjustments necessary for maintaining the status quo (Dahlerup 1987). Although reforms

---

17. Although this book examines current feminist initiatives and the states' responses to them, it is important to note that American feminists first brought male violence against women to the public's attention during the mid-nineteenth century. They did so from the Temperance Platform. Elizabeth Pleck chronicles the history of family violence and public policy in *Domestic Tyranny* (1987).

18. The reasons for this time lag will be explained as this book continues.

may serve this last function, the denial of any amelioration they may offer the oppressed displays a callous indifference to welcomed relief. Indeed, the consequences of reforms in the areas of battery, rape, and sexual harassment can immediately affect women's lives in positive ways that must not be underestimated. This will be made clear from the research presented throughout this work.

A comparative study, such as this one, must contend with several interrelated questions that encompass the policy-making process from initiation to implementation: (1) How do states differentially affect the political cohesion and consciousness of women as a group? (2) What avenues are available for women's claims, and which strategies do women employ to encourage the state's responsiveness to them? (3) Lastly, what are the policy outcomes? The objective is not to provide an exhaustive comparative account of battery, rape, and sexual harassment. Rather, I will have us consider the reasons for significant policy contrasts so as to generate new insights into how states function. In pursuit of that goal, the next chapter provides a comparative historical and cultural context within which we can address the first question concerning the connections between state structure, group cohesion, and political consciousness.

 2

THE COMPARATIVE CONTEXT
State Structures, Cultures, and Movements

To account for the present, one must reflect upon the past. This chapter briefly examines the historical development of each state and those cultural components that are of particular importance in understanding state structure. It also reveals how these factors then influence the shape of political movements in general and feminism in particular.

Swedish women, like their American counterparts, have organized to establish legislative reforms and services for raped, battered and sexually harassed women. Yet, while women in the United States pursue their agenda through an autonomous feminist movement,[1] Swedish women work within the confines of the established political system. The relative absence of an autonomous feminist movement in Sweden can be viewed as a consequence of the structure of the centralized corporatist state. Conversely, federalism in the United States encouraged the presence of an autonomous feminist movement. By looking to the cultural understandings attached to these differences, one may comprehend how differently structured states affect the first and often neglected stage of the policy-making process: how political consciousness arises in those who make claims.

Suffrage: The First Wave of Feminism

A brief examination of the women's suffrage movement in each country provides a logical starting point for examining the effects of state structure on the organization of women's contemporary political claims. Suffrage was the "first independent movement of women for their own liberation" (DuBois 1978, 18). Yet, suffrage,

---

1. The term movement refers to a network of grass-roots organizations that seek to alter public opinion and policy. See note 9 in the previous chapter.

as Ellen Carol DuBois asserts, is rarely accorded the historical recognition it deserves since it is regarded as an isolated institutional reform and not a social movement. The commitment to suffrage was inextricable from feminist demands for other women's rights, however. When approached as a social movement, suffrage provides a striking comparative setting from which to begin an examination of contemporary sexual politics.

Fredrika Bremer, a Swedish suffragist and well-known author, established Europe's first emancipation organization in 1845. Nonetheless, Torild Skard and Elina Haavio-Mannila explain, "The growth of the women's movement in Nordic countries was a gradual affair" (1986, 181). After traveling to the United States in 1849, Bremer returned to Sweden with the belief that American women were more emancipated. Swedish women found her arguments and work so compelling that later, in 1884, they founded a women's organization in her name. The agenda of the association was as broad as it was ambitious: to promote "equal legal, civic, economic and political status for women" (Kälveston 1965, 25). The demand for suffrage was only one facet of this budding feminist movement. Soon, however, feminists and the male political establishment distinguished suffrage from other reforms and gave it prominence.

Six years following the establishment of the Fredrika Bremer Association, suffragists helped to found the Universal Suffrage Association of Sweden. Soon after, both organizations saw the issue of suffrage incorporated within the agendas of the major political parties. The extension of the vote became the leading political cause of both the liberals and socialists. Together, the two parties ensured that all Swedish men were granted the right to vote in 1909, but it was not until 1921 that the all-male and predominantly aristocratic Riksdag granted women's suffrage.

Women's suffrage provides a clear and early example of the cooptation of women's interests. Adams and Winston write that "the suffrage movement as such became indistinguishable from the mainstream of party politics" (1980, 116). Yet for them this signaled something very positive. They write, "The early integration of women activists and women's issues into the major parties helped to overcome the upper class bias in the women's movement" (1980, 116). Given the aristocratic nature of party politics and the outright exclusion of even working-class men, this interpretation is entirely misleading. Although many of the women involved in Fredrika-Bremer and the suffrage movement were the wives and/or daughters of affluent Swedish men, the all-male political parties cannot be credited with deemphasizing the privileged character of the movement. Integrating the initiatives of the women's suffrage movement merely diminished the gendered nature of the fight. "Universal suffrage" immediately became a working-class man's issue; he got the vote first.

Like the Swedish suffragist movement, the agenda of feminists in the United States was broad, particularly in the years prior to the Civil War. Early feminists worked for women's rights in the area of education, property rights, employment opportunities, and the abolition of slavery. "For Black women, suffrage was both a feminist and a racial demand for equality" (Giddings 1985, 159). Yet, as in Sweden, suffrage was soon distinguished from other feminist claims. It became an emblematic guarantee of all other rights.

The American feminist movement was highly decentralized. Women first obtained voting rights and other reforms at the state and local levels. In 1854, Susan B. Anthony encouraged women to petition their state legislatures for suffrage, equal property rights, and guardianship of their children in the case of divorce. Of these demands, suffrage was considered the most radical. It challenged the traditional idea that a woman's interests were identical or at least compatible with those of her father/husband. It is, thus, not surprising that the abolition of slavery eclipsed suffrage as the political rights issue of national importance.

In working for social justice in general and racial justice in particular, women gained invaluable experience. In fact, female anti-slavery societies outnumbered male abolitionist groups. The first anti-slavery organization in the United States was established in 1832 by African American women. A year later, after a group of white women in the American Anti-Slavery Society were forbidden to attend meetings, they too established a society. For white women, anti-slavery activity placed them outside the confines of traditional womanhood (DuBois 1978, 52); for black women, "it was the issue of race that sparked their feminism" (Giddings 1985, 55).

Through anti-slavery societies women not only learned to organize politically but obtained an ideology that described and condemned an oppression seen as analogous to their own. Yet, over fifty years would pass before feminist abolitionists would gain their own suffrage. This was not due to a lack of either strength or political savvy, for they had achieved both during the anti-slavery movement. Unfortunately, white male abolitionists, intent on maintaining political power, also achieved these resources. These men became increasingly reluctant to pursue black male suffrage and women's suffrage as equally important and inseparable demands.[2] They feared that continuing to combine these two issues would mean losing people sympathetic to abolition. Few male abolitionists, therefore, continued to insist on the inextricability of racial and sexual equality.[3]

Eventually, it became clear to feminists that their struggle as women would be dismissed. Elizabeth Cady Stanton wrote a bitter letter to the white male abolitionist Wendell Phillips in which she asks, "Do you believe the African race is composed entirely of males?" (in DuBois 1978, 60). Later outraged by sexual segregation within the World Anti-Slavery Convention in 1840, Stanton decided to work with Lucretia Mott for women's rights. The sexism of the male abolitionists so repelled feminists that they were moved to political autonomy.[4]

In 1848, Stanton and Mott organized the first women's rights convention in Seneca Falls, New York. Most of the women in attendance were white and the daughters and/or wives of affluent white men. Their social status compromised the strength that they might otherwise have achieved through diversity. The relative absence of black women also diminished their claim to represent all women in their fight against male domination. More importantly, Paula Giddings notes that "White feminists often acquiesced to racist ideology, undermining their own cause in doing so" (1985, 6).[5]

Despite this, feminists began to accrue victories at the state and local levels. In 1870, Wyoming adopted women's suffrage, and women there began to serve on juries. Other states soon followed. Women's suffrage organizations throughout the country joined forces and, in 1890, established the National American Woman's Suffrage Association for the specific purpose of obtaining women's

---

2. The struggle for suffrage was not, however, restricted to white women and African Americans. American Jews were also precluded from voting. These restrictions remained legal in Rhode Island until 1842, in North Carolina until 1868, and in New Hampshire until 1877 (Dinnerstein 1994, 15). For a comprehensive examination of anti-Semitism in the United States, see Dinnerstein (1994).

3. By the 1848 Seneca Falls Convention, the only man present to endorse women's suffrage was the African American abolitionist Frederick Douglass.

4. This choice has often occasioned remarks that, for example, American suffragettes had a "preoccupation with maintaining the movement's purity" (Adams and Winston 1980, 125). In choosing to be autonomous from the political establishment, however, the American feminists, like their Swedish counterparts, simply behaved in a manner consistent with their political culture.

5. For a comprehensive history of black women in the United States from the seventeenth century to the contemporary period, see Giddings (1985).

national suffrage.[6] In January 1917, North Dakota granted women the right to vote in presidential elections; shortly after, Ohio, Indiana, Rhode Island and Nebraska did the same. The National American Woman's Suffrage Association then threatened Congress: if it failed to submit a constitutional amendment for women's suffrage, the Association would mobilize against the reelection of those who voted against it. The Association's strategy worked. The Nineteenth Amendment was passed by Congress in January 1918 and took effect in August 1920.

From its inception, the National American Woman's Suffrage Association refused to ally itself with any male political parties. Having been disappointed by both white and black men, suffragists chose not to trust male politicians and activists, whom they suspected would further compromise their demands. Unlike in Sweden, the fight for women's suffrage remained a gendered issue. Suffrage was won not within the political parties but from outside them. After winning the right to vote, American feminists had to chose between integrating into the established political parties and remaining a separate political force. Again, they chose autonomy.

The respective decisions of the American suffragists to remain separate from the male political establishment and of the Swedish suffragists to integrate into it are easily understood from an examination of the development of these states, their structures, and their political cultures.

The United States

A Federalist Republic and Fragmented State

The United States inherited neither a state church nor a centralized bureaucracy from preindustrial or predemocratic times (Skocpol 1985, 12). Though grounded in black slavery, the state had a history of neither feudalism nor monarchy. The authors of *Elites and the Idea of Equality* note, "Citizens had no need to centralize power in order to destroy an existing feudal culture, to challenge the crown, or even to fight large-scale foreign wars—at least for the first 145 years of the country's existence" (Verba, et al., 1987, 42). It was not until the beginning of the twentieth century, when the various

---

6. American feminists noted the success of abolitionists and suspected that a national focus would also work to the advantage of women. Their state and local victories served to further encourage them.

levels of government were partially reorganized, that federal, state, and local governments bureaucratized their administrative functions. In contrast to developments in Sweden, bureaucracy was effectively organized only after the extension of mass suffrage (Orloff 1988, 60).

Despite its eventual bureaucratization, the structure of the United States remained intentionally federalist. Administrative growth, which accelerated with the expansion of state and local government during the New Deal, concerned Americans, who possess an almost instinctive distrust of big government. To ensure that government agencies would be responsible for the proper administration of the law, they were subject to close congressional and judicial oversight at the national level.[7]

The decentralized structure of the American state is apparent at all levels. For example, laws are adopted by both state and national legislatures, though the United States Supreme Court may determine their constitutionality. There are no authoritative central planning agencies; and ambitious civil servants are not assured access to key executive posts. Without a highly centralized state, courts often eclipse bureaucracy in importance as the channels through which grievances are pursued. Public policy planning is dispersed.

The division of sovereignty among different branches of the national government, along with the independence enjoyed by states, local governments, and congressional committees, "help to ensure that state power in the twentieth century United States is fragmented, dispersed and everywhere permeated by organized societal interests" (Skocpol 1985, 12). These interests challenge municipalities, state officials, politicians, and bureaucrats in their assertions of power and expertise. This division of sovereignty and shared powers, intrinsic to federalism, is fundamentally compatible with the heterogeneity of the American people and the political convictions that often serve to unite them.

American Political Culture

The very heterogeneity of the American people that appears to rebuff generalization ironically provides Americans with their identity. For Seymour Martin Lipset, the absence of a feudal past is fundamental:

> Of great significance in facilitating America's development as a nation, both politically and economically, was the fact that the weight

7. Swedish bureaucracy, by contrast, may be questioned by parliament, but oversight remains "unsustained and unsystematic" (Kelman 1981, 108).

of ancient tradition ... was largely absent. It was not only a new nation, it was a new society, much less bound to the customs and values of the past than any nation in Europe. (1967, 107)

Although the social structure was newly created, the political values of the United States clearly were derived from the dissenting side of British political culture. Indeed, the Constitution is best understood as a product of common law, the principles of the Magna Carta, and the liberal philosophy of John Locke.

It is not surprising that Locke's liberalism would appeal to a nation comprised predominantly of immigrants, each group proud of its own culture yet united by a distrust of the various states from which they came.[8] Locke's emphasis on individual sovereignty and limited government accounts for his lasting popularity among many in the United States. He viewed the state as somewhat unnatural—existing only to secure the rights that individual men previously had enjoyed. For Locke, a state that exceeded these bounds was illegitimate.

Populist antagonism towards the state is deeply rooted in American political culture. The essayist Henry David Thoreau expressed this well when he exclaimed

> I heartily accept the motto, "That government is best which governs least"; and I should like to see it acted up to more rapidly and systematically. Carried out, it finally amounts to this, which also I believe: "That government is best which governs not at all." (1970, 109)

Thoreau's emphasis on freedom from state authority accounts for his stature as one of the country's leading liberal intellects.

The ethics of liberalism serves to downplay reliance on a strong government in favor of self-reliance. "Self reliance," writes Stephanie Coontz, "is one of the most cherished American values"—one that has helped to obscure a sexist reality (1992, 69). She explains:

> Self reliance and independence worked for *men* because *women* took care of dependence and obligation. In other words, the liberal theory of human nature and political citizenship did not merely leave women out: It worked precisely because it was applied exclusively to half the population. (Coontz 1992, 53)

---

8. African Americans, by contrast, had even less reason to trust the new nation within which whites had enslaved them. White supremacy in the United States was "further refined into Anglo-Saxon superiority, and the claims of Blacks and Eastern European immigrants (especially Jewish ones) ... were seen to be not only invalid but also dangerous to society" (Giddings 1985, 79). Similarly, Dinnerstein writes: "Despite the venom and hostility displayed toward a variety of European immigrants, especially the Italians, no new group received as much attention and scorn as the east European Jews" (1994, 60).

In general, liberal politics "expunged particularistic ties, social obligations, and personal dependencies from their general operating principles," redefining them as familial (Coontz 1992, 53). Freed from the altruistic concerns of family life, the American emerges as the public man.

American men have long been identified as a diverse group of individuals who possess their own aspirations and find their own means to pursue those aspirations (Hartz 1955; Tocqueville 1956). They are those for whom notions of communal interest are secondary to those of self-interest. They, therefore, prefer a fragmented state, one that legitimizes a proliferation of diverse interests and bears witness to civil society's ability to organize itself. This preference was effectively promoted when the liberal state, unable to claim absolute power, "increasingly disavowed its right to enforce cooperation for some greater good" (Coontz 1992, 56).

Eventually, this political dynamic evolved into a general unwillingness of Americans to trust public authorities to pursue their interests for them (Kelman 1981; Morone 1990; Tocqueville 1956). Given that women are also deeply influenced by masculinist values, they came to accept the tenets of liberalism as valid. American women and men, therefore, actively participate in special interest groups that are generally independent of political parties. They believe such interest groups can best represent their claims. The heavy emphasis on individual achievement paradoxically enhances participation in political interest groups and local communities. While "Swedish communitarianism creates a land of the truly solitary," Heclo and Madsen remark that "American individualism," anomalously, "creates a land of the gregarious" (1987, 22). American individualism spurred competition.

The aspiration for an advantage over opponents and the relatively low value placed on compromise is evidenced by two factors: the numerous nonpartisan interest groups that lobby for their preferred policies, and the high litigation rate. The contemporary feminist movement in the United States provides a striking example of heightened assertiveness, both in its preference for independence from partisan interests and in its reliance on adversarial institutions (i.e., courts) for the resolution of conflicts and adoption of policies beneficial to women.[9]

9. Kelman discusses the predominant involvement of American courts in the resolution of conflicts and the determination of public policy. In Sweden, however, conflicts are avoided and agreements are encouraged. Public policy results from compromises among bureaucratic experts (1981). This will become more apparent as this book continues.

American Feminism: Structural and Cultural Advantages

In the United States, consensus and the avoidance of conflict are not cultural requisites for political expediency. In fact, experts are frequently challenged, protests are common, and conflicts are often enthusiastically approached. American feminists act in accordance with their political culture. Therefore, they have organized a movement that is relatively independent of the state and, at times, unquestionably militant.

Rather than opting for integration within the male political establishment, American feminists often mobilize against it. The American feminist movement remains a protest movement, in part, because the state is too fragmented to successfully integrate it. American political parties, for example, are ideologically less rigid and more pragmatic than their Swedish counterparts. Therefore, they have not been able to redefine women's issues along more traditional political cleavages.

The recognition of American women that their oppression, as women, could provide for an independent feminist movement may, in part, be attributed to the consciousness-raising groups that preceded the movement. Prior to the consciousness-raising groups of the late 1960s and early 1970s, many white feminists within the United States were without a collective identity premised in a recognized experience of domination. Consciousness-raising groups revealed the reality of women's lives as a collective fact, not an isolated event (MacKinnon 1982; 1989).

The ideology of the feminist movement was established out of the communication of women who began to openly discuss their oppression. Formed almost instinctively at first as women gathered in each other's living rooms, the small groups quickly provided a platform for active dissent. Since consciousness-raising groups provided intimacy and support in a forum without structure, they made a brilliant tool for spreading the autonomous, highly decentralized feminist movement. Nonetheless, these groups were not without their problems. The dynamics of structurelessness sometimes caused significant dissension and impeded some political endeavors by failing to acknowledge the power, talent, and knowledge of individual members (Joreen 1973).

The notion that consciousness-raising effectively mobilized women to political action has been challenged by those who assert that there is little empirical evidence either to confirm or to refute its centrality, however. Adams and Winston take this position. They write that such groups were often used "to establish small scale mutual aid projects (e.g., neighborhood daycare) or community service projects (e.g., female health collectives)." They insist that such projects merely served to "maintain group cohesion and solidarity." They conclude that "consciousness raising seems to play its most prominent role in women's groups most inclined to emphasize educational projects and least inclined to political activism" (1980, 131). Adams and Winston, however, fail to appreciate the importance of educational programs as well as women's solidarity and activism outside of the male political establishment. Perhaps their desire to diminish the significance of consciousness-raising groups—and the projects that resulted from them—was driven by their appreciation for Sweden's progressive policies and by their need to explain those policies in the absence of such groups.

While the relative ease with which American women shared their lives with others was conducive to consciousness-raising, we will note that this personalized approach to politics was a cultural anathema in Sweden, where privacy is strongly emphasized. It is not surprising that both consciousness-raising groups and an autonomous feminist movement failed to take root in Sweden.

Unlike their Swedish counterparts, American feminists remained relatively autonomous from the political establishment, refusing to ally themselves with political parties. The following chapters demonstrate that this did not compromise their ability to pursue programs and policies to benefit battered, raped, and sexually harassed women. After all, within federalism, policies often reflect less the will of the majority than bargains struck between a multitude of functionally specialized and relatively autonomous inter-est groups (Adams and Winston 1980; Skocpol 1985). American feminists were, therefore, afforded the opportunity to declare themselves experts on women's conditions. They have formed nonpartisan interest groups, each often focusing on a particular aspect of women's subordination (e.g., 9 to 5, the National Coalition Against Domestic Violence, and Women Against Pornography). Their specialization and autonomy have encouraged the development of unrestrained criticism of the state, and of men generally. Confrontation emerged as a valiant strategy to expand freedom where it had been abridged (Langelan 1993, part one).

The Swedish case provides a striking contrast to the American state and to the political culture and modern feminist movement in the United States.

Sweden

A Centralized, Accommodating, and Expansive State

Although Sweden emerged from a history characterized by sharp cleavages between the rulers and the ruled, the privileges of male aristocrats were dramatically weakened by land confiscations in the late seventeenth century. The transfer of land to peasant ownership was largely the result of state intervention. Thus, the antagonism between male aristocrats and commoners, which came to characterize other European states, was avoided in Sweden early on. Sociologist Erik Allardt insists that such intervention established positive ties between the general population and the state (1986). He argues, moreover, that the transformation of landholding systems is a crucial factor in explaining why the state has "not traditionally been conceived as an oppressive monolith." In fact, "the state has in many respects carried the image of being the benefactor of the common people" (Allardt 1986, 202–203).[10]

The state similarly incorporated the Lutheran Church. Clergymen became state employees. The integration and accommodation of any possible opposition was often achieved through employment. This enhanced the commitment of otherwise inimical factions to the state. The development of a large bureaucratic state capable of providing attractive employment was, in part, "facilitated by a fairly widespread positive public attitude to state intervention" that resulted from the transfer of lands (Allardt 1986, 203). Eventually, state employment secured the consolidation and expansion of centralized state power.

The relative strength of the contemporary Swedish state is reflected in the preparation and implementation of legislative reforms. In Sweden, legislation is adopted at the national level, and the state's bureaucracy is the channel through which legislative reforms are initiated.

The preparation of laws is essentially the task of state-appointed investigatory commissions and/or bureaucrats who work under the direction of a minister. Indeed, ministries often give commissions

---

10. Yet while male nobles were deprived of many of their landholdings, they did retain their right to public office. Thus during the early eighteenth century, nearly 80 percent of Swedish nobles earned their living as public officials. The nobility's grip on public affairs lasted well over a century. It was not until 1883 that Sweden had a nonaristocratic, male prime minister. Even then, he was appointed by the King, who continued to select prime ministers until 1905. From then on, the Riksdag chose them.

and bureaucrats directives "which outline the problems to be considered, the goals to be achieved, and sometimes even the approaches to take to reach these conditions" (Peterson 1977, 48). Swedish legislative committees and bureaucrats frequently carry out detailed inquiries, the results of which are presented in official investigatory reports (*Statens offentliga utredningar*, SOU). Such a report provides a general justification for any proposed legislative reforms. It is then scrutinized by the minister's legal department, which sends the work out for written comments from interested authorities and organizations. This part of the process is called "remiss." This formal solicitation of alternative viewpoints channels debate.[11] Remiss provide concerned parties the opportunity to raise any possible objections, apprehensions, or comments before the ministry proceeds. If the ministry and other cabinet members then decide to pursue the reform, the government submits a refined draft of the bill to the appropriate standing committee within the Riksdag. The committee reviews the proposed legislation and issues a report, containing its opinion of the bill, to a plenary session of the Riksdag for a vote.

By the time the Riksdag considers a bill, parliamentary majorities are relatively easy to obtain, as governments emerge from disciplined party majorities that can ensure that their legislation is usually passed. And, legislative debates are less common in Sweden than in the United States. When they do occur, it is only after a commission report or proposed reform is made public. By then the ministry has come out with a well-thought-out proposal and a defense against any possible criticisms (Premfors 1983). Peterson, a political analyst, notes that "in delaying and channeling public criticism, and by forcing it to deal with a comprehensive and technically imposing proposal, commissions make subsequent political opposition much more difficult" (1977, 49–50).[12]

While laws may be appealed, appeals are brought to the ministerial cabinet that first drafted the law, not to the courts. In addition,

---

11. The process contains three tiers. There are state authorities who are required to comment on a particular law. Other relevant authorities and organizations receive the report and/or the bill and are provided the opportunity to respond. Lastly, ordinary citizens have the right to submit their views. One should note a diminished level of influence from the first to last tier.

12. Similarly, Eva Tiby, a Swedish feminist lawyer, likens the remiss process to a washing machine. She writes, "Political conflicts and oppositions are washed clean through a system of report studies and comment circulation ... After the political question is washed long enough, out comes a so-called non-partial, objective and irreproachable law" (1987, 24).

complaints regarding ill enforcement of a law are channeled through a government-appointed ombudsman who has authority only to reprimand. Sweden, therefore, lacks a powerful and autonomous avenue through which citizens can bring charges against the state. Dissatisfied constituents are impeded in their pursuit of greater political accountability. This situation underlines the imposing authority and centralization of the Swedish state.

Swedish Political Culture

While in the United States it is important to win conflicts, in Sweden it is important to avoid them.[13] Comparative studies have shown that Swedish politicians and bureaucrats are distinguished from their foreign counterparts by the considerable stress they place on social skills and collegiality. Swedes prefer to yield rather than fight, even when they suspect that they are right. These characteristics are components of what Åke Daun, the well-known Swedish ethnologist, refers to as "the Swedish mentality" (1989).

In contrast to their American counterparts, even Sweden's political elite prefers consensus to conflict and generally does not exploit advantages. Few have captured the etiquette of Sweden's elite as well as Thomas Anton, who writes:

> Swedish officials prefer to pull rather than push, avoid confrontations, are generous when ahead and accommodating when behind less because they are humane individuals ... than because they perceive the potential consequences for *themselves* that can arise from different styles of action. (1980, 296)

The pressure to conform is great. While noting that conformity is present throughout Scandinavia, Erik Allardt insists that it "seems to be most visible in Sweden" (1986, 212). The penalty for those who either refuse or prove too socially inept for this etiquette is ostracism and alienation from political life.

Relative to the United States, Sweden is ethnically and culturally homogeneous. Historian Hans Fredrik Dahl argues that Nordic countries generally score "comparatively low on 'pluralism,' on their ability to tolerate alternatives and to allow a multiplicity of groups and opinions to blossom" (1986, 108). This does not necessarily mean that dissenters meet with overt oppression. As Allardt explains, they "are not hindered in expressing and practicing their

---

13. A list of numerous psychological tests and interviews that substantiate this assertion may be found in Daun (1989).

views, but they are often disregarded by the political organizations and the media" (1986, 211). Heclo and Madsen elaborate on this point. They assert that the Swedish system necessitates social consanguinity as a prerequisite for political recognition. They write:

> Any individual not playing by the rules of group interaction is essentially alone and vulnerable, with no place to go. There is simply no alternative mechanism to commission work, no alternative structures of corporate representation, no alternative processes for getting along in public life. (1987, 21–22)

Therefore, even Sweden's feminists "play by the rules."

Swedish Feminism: Structural and Cultural Constraints

Maud Eduards, the Swedish political scientist, writes that most women's organizations

> have sought to avoid conflict in favor of adoption and "respectability" in a resistant and male-dominated political structure.... The majority of women political activists work within established political institutions which have always been dominated by men. (1989, 15–16)

Many feminists work for reforms within governmental bureaucracies or women's sections of parties rather than in autonomous women's projects and organizations.

Political parties, in particular, have been "remarkably efficient in coopting both women and women's demands" (Eduards 1989, 16). Four of the five major parties contain specific women's sections that act as women's interest groups *within* the parties. Each section then defers to the "larger" party agenda (Haavio-Mannila, et al., 1985).[14] Party discipline has conventionally been so acute that (male-dominated) parties control candidate nominations and determine which policies to promote and which to ignore. Women's interests have, thus, been subsumed by gender-neutral approaches to sex equity. Consequently, a higher proportion of women in the Riksdag has not translated into a greater commitment to policies that would radically alter male dominance (Eduards 1992; Elman 1993a). To the contrary, once incorporated in the political establishment, women are "pitted against women, as champions of the established order" (Eduards 1992, 98). As one

---

14. The one exception is the Left Party (formerly the Communist Party), which has tried to incorporate women into the party by insisting that women's concerns are inextricable from other issues.

woman active in Swedish politics stated in a television interview, "I am first a Social Democrat, and after that a woman" (in Eduards 1992, 98). The loyalty that women have traditionally extended to parties has compromised the effectiveness with which they could otherwise collaborate and mobilize to achieve common objectives (Hernes 1988).

While Heclo and Madsen portray a rather constraining political system that necessitates agreement to the pre-existing rules of the game, Helga Hernes offers an alternative perspective. She insists that the political culture expresses a "more benign view of the state as an instrument of popular will." She then concludes that:

> Scandinavian feminists act in accordance with their own political culture in turning to the state, even in those instances where they wish to build alternative institutions. (1988, 204–5)[15]

While feminists in the United States hold a more cynical, if not contemptuous, view of the state, Swedish feminists are less anti-state. It is impossible, however, to determine whether it is their "more benign view of the state" that sustains their trust in it or, as Heclo and Madsen suggest, they simply have no other alternatives.

As mentioned earlier, numerous outsiders have noted the absence of a feminist movement in Sweden, yet few have grasped the contempt with which self-proclaimed feminists are regarded. Hilda Scott, however, is exceptional in her ability to perceive and explain the hostility directed against feminists. She writes:

> There is probably no Western country where hostility to "feminism" as opposed to "women's liberation" is so out of proportion to the strength and militancy of the avowed feminists in the women's movement. (1982, 158)[16]

---

15. The German critic Hans Magnus Enzenberger's observations echo those of Hernes: "Swedish citizens are always willing to comply with their authorities with such naivete and trust[,] as if the benevolence of the authorities were beyond question" (in Zetterberg 1986, 92).

16. Scott distinguishes between women's liberationists and feminists. She defines feminists as women who "see women as oppressed and men as oppressors and believe that the radical reordering of society ... requires the recognition of this major conflict and its resolution" (1982, 158). Scott's definition of feminists is consistent with my own.

Alternatively, women's liberationists, some of whom regard themselves as feminists, often attribute women's oppression to factors other than patriarchy. These women are incorporated into various male parties and organizations to oppose other forms of oppression whose eradication they believe would benefit women. For example, this would include opposition to class exploitation.

She notes that it is neither the demands of feminists nor their desire to help women to which the society so vehemently objects; it is, instead, their construed unwillingness to conform to the Swedish tradition of conciliation (1982, 159).

While many Swedes may object to feminism because it is conflict-oriented, feminism does not create conflict as much as it acknowledges its existence by exposing the oppressive conditions under which women live. This very act of exposure leads to the accusation of creating conflict. In a culture that places a premium on conflict avoidance and the maintenance of borders between public and private life, it is easy to understand the Swedes' strong aversion to feminism.

Sexual politics, then, poses an interesting challenge to the Swedish state and to its policy makers, who, having long been credited with establishing a base of economic security for Swedes, are frequently unwilling to acknowledge that issues of inequality persist. Torild Skard and Elina Haavio-Mannila note that "At a time when the women's liberation movement was sending shock waves throughout the United States and the rest of the industrialized world, social scientists in the Nordic countries began a gender-role debate ..." The debate focused on "the two roles of women—in the family and in the labor force—and how they should be combined" (1986, 183). Scholars continue to argue that state policy should facilitate combining women's "roles." So instead of a feminist movement, women in Sweden witnessed a proliferation of "expert" opinions concerning women's double burden.

Summary

While Swedish activists increasingly became part of the state, American feminists mobilized against it while seeking concessions from it. American feminists consciously avoided the partisan alliances and state affiliations upon which their Swedish counterparts are so dependent. Rather than opting for integration within the male political establishment, the modern feminist movement in the United States pursued a strategy of sisterhood as had the suffragists before them. This strategy stressed the recognition that "all women, no matter how diverse they are in other respects, share the common problems of their sex" (Adams and Winston 1980, 132). This consciousness and the resultant cohesiveness of American feminists helped make their claims relatively resistant to cooptation into other policy areas like labor, and family.[17] Thus, the federalist structure of the American state was further deprived of its cooptive strength. It simply could not embody women's gender-specific issues as partisan, labor or family issues as did the corporatist structure of the Swedish state.

---

17. Annie McCombs suggests that this same consciousness and cohesion also renders the movement resistant to criticism of class bias and racism (related in conversation, 9 September 1993).

3

STATE INTERVENTION AND WOMAN BATTERY

Women in both Sweden and the United States have organized to establish legislative reforms and services for abused women. As noted in the last chapter, Swedish feminists rely upon partisan alliances and state bureaucracies to further the interests of women. This strategy relies upon the willingness of Swedish activists to accept the constraints of the established political system, which determines what is politically expedient. It also indicates that, within the centralized corporatist state, there are few alternatives for feminists outside of the established political process.

By contrast, American feminists pursue their agenda through an autonomous women's movement. This reflects their hesitance to align with male-dominated political institutions (e.g., parties) which would mandate compromising feminist goals. As well, it denotes the greater political access available to women within federalism. Yet, cast upon its own resources, can an autonomous feminist movement within a federalist state constitute a formidable interest group through which feminist policies result? Or, are the compromises that corporatist integration necessitates, in the end, more favorable to women?

To answer these questions, I begin with an overview of common problems for battered women and the emergence of political claims to redress those problems. I then examine avenues through which activists in each state pursued the adoption of services and reforms to provide battered women relief. Finally, I contrast and evaluate the results of their efforts.

It is vital to understand that woman battery is neither marginal nor episodic in either state. While it is recognized that woman battery is epidemic in the United States, in Sweden there is a greater reticence to address the problem.[1] In 1967, the United States Task

---

1. The reasons for this were alluded to in the second chapter and will be further discussed here. Additionally, while there are numerous American studies pertaining to woman battery, in Sweden there is a dearth of research on the issue. To date there have only been two doctoral works on the topic (Bergman 1987; Hydén 1992). Feminists

Force on Crime noted that injury inflicted by intimates is more serious than injury inflicted by strangers (U.S. President's Commission on Law Enforcement and the Administration of Justice 1967, 15). Similarly, and more recently, Sweden's Statistics Bureau noted that "violence that takes place in the victim's home is the most serious." The Bureau noted that 33 percent of these acts resulted in a visit to a physician and 17 percent resulted in at least a one-week sick leave from work (Statistics Sweden 1981).

Woman battery accounts for between 33 and 50 percent of all police calls in the United States (Morgan 1984, 707) and nearly 25 percent of all reported assaults in Sweden (Leander 1989, 48). Alarming as these statistics are, authorities in both countries concede that under-reporting remains a serious analytic problem.[2] These statistics, therefore, are probably low. Not only do estimations of the problem remain conservative; they fail to capture the horror of the abuse itself. Indeed, the abuse is often so severe that the strongest reason for a woman staying with her assailant is, paradoxically, the fear of what the batterer will do if she attempts to leave (Elman and Eduards 1991; Martin 1976).

The Federal Bureau of Investigation reports that every four days a woman is beaten to death in the United States by a man she knows (Toufexis 1987). Approximately 30 percent of all women murdered in the United States were killed by their husbands or boyfriends (Becker, Bowman, and Torrey 1994, 559). In Sweden, a woman is killed under such circumstances every ten days (Justitiedepartementet 1991, 19) accounting for 60 percent of all female homicide (Johansson 1991).[3] When one considers these statistics, the fear battered women have of their assailants is not irrational. Nonetheless, this femicidal reality has often been "implicitly denied by the common view of feminists and non-feminists that rape and

---

strongly objected to Bo Bergman's dissertation when, on the basis of 22 interviews with battered women in hospital emergency rooms, he depicted most of the women as mentally imbalanced. For an in-depth critique, read Lundgren and Eriksen (1988). Margareta Hydén's work, *Woman Battering as Marital Act: The Construction of a Violent Marriage*, provides interviews with batterers and their victims to understand how each "made sense of the violent action" (1992, 12). She presents the perspectives of perpetrator and victim as equally valid and implies that women are responsible for the violence committed against them.

2. Indeed, statistics obtained from battered women's shelters throughout Sweden showed that 75 percent of those seeking shelter assistance had not reported their abusers to the police (*Dagens Nyheter*, 29 May 1992).

3. Criminologists speculate that places with lower crime rates generally indicate a higher rate of woman abuse.

battery are the most extreme forms of violence against women" (Radford and Russell 1992, xiv).[4]

Given the grave danger in which batterers place their victims, it is not surprising that in both Sweden and the United States most efforts on behalf of battered women have centered on establishing and maintaining shelters; a safe place to stay is always the most immediate and pressing need of battered women. Although shelters are staffed by committed volunteers, activists also favor the use of paid staff to ensure that women who could not otherwise afford to volunteer become actively involved. Taken together, staff salaries and housing expenses make shelters costly and funding a constant concern. The battered women's movement, unlike many other movements, cannot subsist on the financial support of its constituents. In both countries, and to varying degrees, activists turned to the state for fiscal assistance.

The United States

Autonomous Shelters

In the United States, the first shelter for battered women was established by a feminist legal-aid collective that evolved from a consciousness-raising group in St. Paul, Minnesota. In 1972, the collective had begun a crisis telephone line in the county Legal Aid office. The line was financed by contributions from women throughout the community. The group soon discovered that battered women were essentially homeless if they decided to leave their assailants. Responding to the problem, members of the collective simply took battered women into their own homes until they could find them a place of their own and a means of self-support. Two years later, these same activists were able to purchase their own house for battered women with private funds. Numerous other shelters across the nation began in precisely the same way.[5]

The feminist movement provided the structural foundation upon which the battered women's movement was built (Freeman 1975; Tierney 1982). Older feminist groups, such as the National

---

4. The authors provide a startling political analysis of woman-killing that relocates "femicide within the continuum of sexual violence and establishes its significance in terms of sexual politics" (Radford and Russell 1992, 4).

5. For an inventory of the country's first shelters (1972–1976) and how they began, see Del Martin (1976), Chapter 10.

Organization for Women, played a crucial role. Many feminists in the legal, mental-health, and health-care professions provided a pre-existing network of experienced activists. More importantly, several who became involved with the issue of battery had considerable experience in working on other women's issues. As feminists, they opposed all manifestations of patriarchy, including hierarchy and the traditional political system. Consequently, they stressed self-help for battered women.

For American feminists, the importance of women's shelters took on an ideological significance that was largely absent in Sweden. Shelters were seen as providing women a remedy that was largely independent of a patriarchal state. Unlike Swedish feminists, who generally possess a more favorable view of the state's ability to provide women services, American feminists remained more skeptical of the state's capacity to rectify gender inequality. Betsy Warrior, one of the foremost feminist activists involved with the battered woman's movement, exemplifies this anti-state perspective:

> Laws against wife beating aren't the solution to this problem, ... The only short-term solution that is possible is the establishment of houses that could serve as refuges ... Because of the public attitude of apathy—which connotes tacit acceptance of crimes against women—we can't look to social agencies to set up such refuges but must find ways of establishing them ourselves. (1976, 20–21)

American activists, therefore, established shelters without state funding. They purchased private property with money they received from numerous individuals, fund-raisers, and foundation grants.

Within five years there were approximately 250 shelters throughout the United States. The National Coalition Against Domestic Violence (NCADV) was established the following year to unite a majority of them. According to Betsy Warrior, author of *Battered Women's Directory* (1985), there were as many as 1,100 shelters nationwide offering services ranging from counseling to legal advocacy, childcare, and occupational training.[6] More recently, *Ms.* magazine reports that there are nearly 1,500 shelters throughout the United States (1994, 54).

Although American feminists were undoubtedly skeptical of the state, they did argue that it should not be absolved of its responsibilities to protect and provide for all its citizens. In fact, Warrior and others later expressed concern that the battered women's movement

---

6. This figure does not include crisis lines and safe-home networks operating independently of shelters and the National Coalition Against Domestic Violence.

was taking on too many responsibilities with too few resources. They suggested that:

> A shelter should deliberately put limitations on the services it is willing to provide. Instead of allowing communities to shift the burden of providing medical, legal and economic assistance, and housing onto the meager resources of shelters, communities should be expected to provide these services for all who need them. (Warrior 1985, 158)

The battered women's movement believed that the state should take some financial responsibility for the services activists provide.

Gradually, activists turned to the state, but primarily out of financial necessity. Yet, while state money solved some problems, it created others. As Susan Schechter, author of *Women and Male Violence* (1982), explains: "A larger funding base sometimes undermined important movement principles" (1988, 305). The deeply egalitarian, committed, and collective nature of the movement receded. Shelters began to resemble social service agencies within which professionals were employed with state funds to serve "clients." Battered women were increasingly assigned the position of "victim" (Schechter 1988, 306), a term feminists earlier avoided in their attempts to promote the notion that while women battery is pervasive, it must be challenged and *survived.* Nonetheless, the victim label entitles women to "remedies the state can provide" (Matthews 1994, 159). Patricia Williams, a professor of law, exposes this predicament when she sadly remarks that she "learned that the best way to give voice to those whose voice had been suppressed was to argue that they had no voice" (1991, 156).

The success that so many activists had in soliciting state funds led to the need to expand their services. However, the ability of feminist activists to meet women's needs became increasingly difficult as funding became harder to obtain. As a result, many projects have been forced to turn battered women away.[7]

The recession and shift from domestic to military spending during the 1980s resulted in a fierce competition between different social services for scarce resources. Activists noted that too great a financial dependence on state and local authorities could be disastrous. They stressed the importance of diversified funding in the event that something happens to a particular source. In fact, the

---

7. In their brochure, the National Coalition Against Domestic Violence estimates that for every woman accepted into a shelter, two others are turned away (undated, "Every 15 seconds a woman is battered in this country," received October 1994).

Center for Women Policy Studies in Washington, D.C. has compiled research on shelters across the country, and the center's policy experts indicate that shelters depend on private sources as their largest funding category and prefer this funding alternative.[8] This is not to say that shelters do not want to receive government funding. They are simply reluctant to accept it when it means a consequential loss of their autonomy (Matthews 1994; Schechter 1988).

The battered women's movement developed innovative ways to meet its financial needs. For example, some battered women's coalitions have successfully lobbied their states (twenty-one of them) to adopt a bill to increase the marriage license fee by a specified sum; these additional revenues go to battered women's shelters and projects (Lerman and Livingston 1983, 4). Such legislation creates an ongoing source of funding and provides a solution when government funding is limited. Other states have adopted legislation that imposes fines on men convicted of woman-battery; these monies are then used to fund services for battered women. Like the marriage license fee, this legislation provides for a continued funding source largely independent of annual political struggles associated with the budgetary process.

Nearly all shelters receive some governmental support from their state and local communities. Thirty-seven states have appropriated funding specifically for shelters and the direct services they provide (Gelb 1983, 253). In addition to taxing marriage licenses and collecting fines from batterers, state funding is secured through state agencies such as departments of social services. Additionally, shelters may receive financial assistance directly from state (e.g., gubernatorial) and local (e.g., mayoral) budgets.[9]

Yet, relative to Sweden, the American shelter movement still has greater autonomy from the state. This is exemplified, in part, by the existence of numerous programs, shelters, and lobbying groups that have no affiliation to political parties or government bureaucracies. Moreover, the shelters' frequent preference for, and reliance on, private funds and volunteerism is not unusual for American service

---

8. This information was related to me through a telephone conversation with Lois Copeland, 15 April 1991. During this time she served as a publications manager for the Center for Women Policy Studies. The reports to which she referred are those contained within the Center's policy journal, entitled *Response*.

9. Because of the diverse ways in which American shelters obtain governmental support, it is nearly impossible to compare budgetary data for the United States and Sweden. Support for battered women is often part of other anti-crime, victim service appropriations. More recently, financial assistance has been made available through President Clinton's 1994 Crime Bill.

providers. For example, many of them, including hospitals, utilize volunteers. Thus, placed within a larger sociopolitical context, the position of shelters is hardly unique.

Sweden

State-Sanctioned Shelters

Unlike their American counterparts, Swedish women, at the outset, petitioned the state for public housing and funding with which to establish shelters and services for battered women. Indeed, they did so with little hesitation. Even today, projects for battered women are entirely financed by the state, although the resources that they receive are meager.

Sweden's shelter movement began five years after the first American shelters opened. The first Swedish shelter opened in 1979, in Gothenburg; later that same year another opened in Stockholm. There are presently nearly ninety shelters and thirty-five separate crisis lines incorporated by the National Organization of Emergency Shelters for Battered Women in Sweden (ROKS),[10] established in 1984. Despite the distinction between crisis lines and shelters, authorities frequently refer to all projects against woman battery as shelters. Consequently, many falsely assume that all of Sweden's 125 projects are shelters for battered women.

That Sweden's shelters opened five years after American shelters began is explained, in part, by Birgitta Wistrand, a former president of the Frederika Bremer Association, a national women's rights organization. She writes, "The ideas behind the movement for women's rights and emancipation have their sources abroad" (1981, 10). It is also worth noting that neither crisis lines nor safe-home networks preceded the shelters.[11] There was simply no feminist movement to provide the foundation of the battered women's movement.

Since most of Sweden's first battered women's activists had neither participated in consciousness-raising groups nor been in the women's movement, they lacked the social and political solidarity of

10. ROKS is the Swedish acronym for *Riksorganisationen för kvinnojourer i Sverige*.
11. Safe-home networks are an alternative to the costly provision of shelters. They consist of women who are able to volunteer a temporary haven (often their own homes) to battered women. A major disadvantage of safe-homes, however, is that the community of women that one finds in a shelter is missing. There is usually only one woman in a safe-home at any time. Relative to a shelter, however, it is a low-cost service model that provides women safety while they seek legal advice and crisis counseling.

their American counterparts. In fact, Swedish battered women's activists strenuously objected to feminism from the start. The establishment of one of Sweden's first shelters, the All Women's House, in Stockholm, serves to illustrate this point.

Those who began the Stockholm shelter were indirectly affiliated with the Social Democratic Party, which intervened on their behalf to oppose feminists who had worked for three years to obtain a center for all women, not only for those who were battered. One of the reasons the founders of the shelter objected to the feminists was the latter's politics and the presence of lesbians among its membership. The women who founded the shelter were operating out of a more conventional social-service approach to battered women. The party eventually secured the house that was to be the women's center and gave it to the battered women's advocates. Despite the fact that the primary goal of the advocates was to service battered women, they referred to the shelter as the All Women's House. Thus, they rhetorically countered the feminist claim that only a women's center (and not a shelter) would be open to *all* women. The resultant lack of political and social solidarity among activists made them vulnerable to state intervention. The Social Democratic Party was able to arbitrate the disagreements among women. The unfortunate consequence of this bitter struggle was that many feminists were alienated from the shelter movement.[12]

The Swedish shelters differed from their American counterparts in their origins and in their source of funding. They also differed in the absence of safe-home networks. Sweden lacked an autonomous feminist movement. The political battle to establish its first shelter divided women, thus destroying the requisite cohesiveness necessary to establish a network of safe-homes. Perhaps more importantly, Swedish women appeared to expect the state to provide such resources. Consequently, activists did not assume personal responsibility for the battered women in their community as did their American counterparts.

Nearly all of Sweden's shelters receive funding from local councils and/or from social welfare departments. However, the response from local councils varies. Only one-third of the councils financially

---

12. Feminists in the United States, particularly those who are lesbians, have also been alienated by anti-feminists within the shelter movement (Schechter 1982). However, relative to the Swedish state, the American state has been less able to dictate the outcomes of these conflicts. This is because, as I argued in the previous chapter, maintaining autonomy from the state has been a crucial aspect of American political culture, including the feminist movement.

supports battered women shelters (Eduards 1992, 92). This funding primarily covers rental costs. The property of Stockholm's All Women's House, for example, is owned by the Stockholm City Council; the Stockholm Department of Welfare pays the rent. Such rental schemes are common for nonprofit service providers within the welfare state. From a distance, these arrangements appear ideal. A closer examination of the state's responsiveness to the shelters, however, provides a somewhat less impressive portrait.

Although some shelter activists are available on a twenty-four-hour emergency basis through the police and social services, all Swedish shelters and crisis lines maintain limited hours. Even the crisis line at the All Women's House, one of the country's oldest shelters, only operates evenings between six and nine. These are not the most effective hours of operation, considering that men are most likely to batter women between five and eleven at night (Gelles 1972, 100–105). Ulla Britt Forsberg, a coordinator of the All Women's House, realizes that the house and its lines should be accessible on a twenty-four-hour basis to be fully effective (interview, 1988). Increased funding would enhance the operational stability of this and other shelters but suggested increases compete with calls to cut social spending. To date, no clear resolution of this problem has emerged.

Sweden's few employed shelter personnel usually maintain part-time positions working between five to thirty hours a week. These positions are indirectly funded through a government employment program (*lönebidrag*) similar to American CETA.[13] Unlike the United States, however, few, if any, shelters employ staff through private funding. While funding is a concern of shelters and projects, active solicitation of private funding in Sweden is highly unusual. Unlike their counterparts, Swedish shelters and projects expect to rely fully on the state to provide sufficient public services, including necessary shelter expenses. This expectation may, in part, arise from the higher taxes citizens are required to pay.

The majority of women who do not work as state-funded employees work as volunteers. The heavy reliance on volunteers makes it difficult to extend staffing hours, particularly during the day,

---

13. In 1962, CETA (Comprehensive Employment and Training Act) was established as a job-training program that offered public employment under the Department of Labor. It was a major source of federal funding for the staff salaries of battered women's projects; until its elimination during the Reagan administration, it probably funded more battered women's shelters and projects than any other federal agency.

when many activists work at other jobs. According to Ebon Kram, coordinator of ROKS, the national office receives calls from all over Sweden simply because it is open during the day (interview, 1990). Unfortunately, answering crisis calls makes it difficult for ROKS to pursue its administrative tasks, which include training activists, educating the community at large on woman abuse, and lobbying for legislation beneficial to abused women. ROKS has been pursuing additional funds to enlarge its staff since its inception in 1984. It was not until 1988 that it was able to obtain enough funding for a small office and a full-time office worker. The government again increased monies for measures to counter violence against women in 1991 and is likely to do so again. ROKS is now able to employ its director.

While the heavy reliance on volunteers makes it difficult to provide sufficient services to women in need, state agencies such as the National Council for Crime Prevention (BRÅ)[14] insist that battered women's projects must continue to utilize volunteers (Naumann 1988). Yet, while activists on behalf of battered women are expected to volunteer and funding is claimed to be scarce, men's crisis centers enjoy large state allocations. From 1986 to 1987, for example, over 100 battered women's projects received 890,000 Swedish krowns (ca. $136,000 U.S.), while seven men's centers and crisis lines received 730,000 Swedish krowns (ca. $112,000 U.S.) (*Kvinnobulletinen* 1987, 32).

Although volunteerism is not unusual in other countries, including the United States, it is rare in Sweden. Sweden's commitment to social democracy results in an emphasis on paid labor. Relative to other countries, Sweden has fewer charities. Taxes are progressive and unusually high, and the state is expected to provide for its citizens. Ebon Kram notes that prior to Sweden's social welfare system, the oppressed depended on charity—"that was in the 1800s, and that is the situation for women today" (interview, 1990). The shelters are unique in this regard. Volunteerism is viewed contemptuously, and no other service sector depends so thoroughly upon it.

---

14. BRÅ is the Swedish acronym for *Brottsförebyggande rådet*.

The Criminal Justice Systems: Common Obstacles

Although providing women shelter is the primary goal of activists in each country, they also have made efforts to reform the criminal justice system. They seek the institution of new policies that reflect the serious criminal nature of woman battery and provide women with protection. The goal of these efforts is to eliminate the system's traditional avoidance and disdain for woman abuse cases and to ensure that the laws are enforced as vigorously as if the involved parties were total strangers.

Traditionally, American legal doctrine officially sanctioned a husband's assault upon his wife. Battery was declared an acceptable practice as long as the instrument of assault (whip or rattan) was no thicker than the batterer's thumb (*Bradley v. State*, 1824). A half-century later, a North Carolina court ruled that, in the absence of permanent injury or excessive violence, "it is better to draw the curtains, shut out the gaze, and leave the parties to forget and forgive" (*State v. Oliver*, 1874). Similarly, Swedish laws authorized men to beat their wives, and, until 1864, there were no restraints imposed upon men for doing so. Although woman battery is no longer legally sanctioned by either country, the insensitivity of many to the harm that women endure lingers and is embedded in the criminal justice system's response to it.

In both the United States and Sweden, the criminal justice system neglected to provide battered women adequate protection and trivialized the violence that women endure. Police departments attached low priority to calls from battered women and routinely failed to advise them of their right to file a report or to have their batterers detained and/or arrested (Elman and Eduards 1991; Ferraro 1989). Prosecutors were similarly remiss and preferred mediation and conciliation to criminal action. This approach had "the effect of depreciating the severity of the complaints" and transformed "patterns of repetitive, serious, violent behavior into social disturbances, family spats, or quarrels" (Eisenberg and Micklow 1977, 60). The reluctance of prosecutors to pursue criminal avenues of redress was exacerbated by women's fear of prosecuting their spouses. Thus, in both states, cases of woman battery rarely ended up in court (Jahn 1987; U.S. Commission on Civil Rights 1982, 36).

Whatever the problems of getting to court, once there, battered women are confronted by judges who are equally insensitive to their needs. For example, in 1987, a judge in Massachusetts castigated a battered wife for "wasting his time" when she appeared before him seeking an order of protection. The same woman was later killed by the man from whom she was seeking protection (Goodman 1982).[15] More recently, a Swedish judge ruled that men have the right to batter "uppity women" (Bodström 1989).

Even on those rare occasions when men actually receive sentences for their crimes, in both countries the penalties for women batterers are significantly lower than for individuals who batter men (Attorney General's Task Force on Family Violence 1984, 12; Jahn 1987). While a comparative analysis of convictions and sentences is impossible,[16] one can examine efforts taken within each state to protect women and treat their beatings as a significant criminal offense.

The American Case

From the beginning, American feminists turned to the law to redress the frustrations of battered women. This is not surprising when one considers that the modern feminist movement emerged from the civil rights movement. The civil rights movement placed a tremendous emphasis on the legal system as both a means of social control and a vehicle for political transformation.[17] Not unlike African American activists, feminists attempted to transform their oppression through legal means. Because legal reform can be approached through litigation by interest groups and individuals from outside the established political system, such activism was consistent with the anti-state bias of the American battered women's movement.

Model state laws for abused women also have been introduced, however. These were often authored by battered women's advocates

---

15. Her death sparked such protest that the judge was placed under investigation and all of the state's 150 district court judges were mandated to attend educational programs on woman abuse. Within one year complaints of woman battery quadrupled as a result of the publicity given the training programs (*New York Times*, 3 May 1987).

16. In both countries, woman battery is classified as "assault," a gender-neutral crime. More importantly, efforts at comparison are obstructed because Swedish courts do not maintain a record of the sexes of perpetrators and victims.

Even within each state, an analysis of the penalties batterers receive is complicated. Unlike any other crime victim, battered women sometimes want lower sentences and penalties for their assailants because they may be financially and/or emotionally dependent on them or may simply fear retaliation. Nonetheless, feminists in both countries caution that a reduction in charges and penalties for cases of woman battery may serve to confirm the prevailing attitudes that woman beating is not a serious crime.

17. For a more detailed analysis of this duality, see Williams (1991), particularly Chapter 8.

who, together with other political actors, such as governors, Congress members, or bureaucrats, could introduce laws for legislative consideration. Yet because the American system requires separate elections for the executive and legislative branches at the national, state, and local levels, members of these legislative bodies are subject to interest-group pressure that serves to further limit party discipline. Consequently, bills often generate publicity and public reaction at a very early stage so that, when they reach the floor, passage is not assured. Moreover, because legislators with divergent views must come to agreement on a bill, the final legislation may be quite different from the original proposal.

Legislative obstacles forced many within the battered women's movement to seek legal reform first through litigation. A series of Supreme Court decisions opened the way for numerous liability suits against public authorities.[18] As a result, battered women were able to sue law enforcement agencies and others for negligence.

The first of these civil suits was brought in 1976 against the Oakland, California, police department (*Scott v. Hart*, 1976). Advocates on behalf of battered women argued that the police department's arrest-avoidance policies violated the equal protection clause of the Fourteenth Amendment. The department refused to respond to women assaulted in their homes even though it responded to victims of violence in other settings. That same year, lawyers in New York City took action, on behalf of twelve battered women, against the city police department on similar grounds (*Bruno v. Codd*, 1977). In both cases, the courts recognized the claims of the women as valid and ordered the police departments to change their policies to acknowledge the criminal dimensions of woman battery.

These cases, publicized by feminist lawyers, provided a model for later suits (Woods 1978; 1981). One more recent and notorious

18. As early as 1961, the United States Supreme Court decided that a federal statute (42 U.S.C. sec. 1983) could be used to provide litigants the right to sue in federal court for damages caused by the improper conduct of a government official, including a police officer, when that conduct violated the constitution. In 1978, the Court extended this right to include municipalities and government agencies themselves. In 1980, the Court reasoned that since individual police officers and government officials are protected from personal liability while fulfilling their duties, local governments may be required to pay damages for incidents in which their conduct resulted in constitutional violations. In a more recent and related finding, the Court ruled that cities are potentially liable for inadequate police training when it displays a deliberate indifference to the rights of the public (*Canton Ohio v. Harris*, 1989). This last ruling provided an even greater impetus for police departments to update their manuals and other training regarding the serious nature and criminality of woman abuse.

case was brought by Tracey Thurman, a battered woman, against the city of Torrington, Connecticut, in 1985. It was the first time a federal judge had permitted a suit against a municipality on the grounds that the police force had violated a woman's Constitutional rights by providing her less protection than complainants in other cases not involving domestic violence. The jury found that the police did not do enough to protect Ms. Thurman from her husband and awarded her more than $2 million in compensatory damages. The implications of this case were extensive. The case set a federal precedent demonstrating the high cost to municipalities whose law enforcement agencies do not provide adequate protection to battered women.

Shortly after the Thurman ruling, a federal court of appeals found that while the police normally cannot be held liable for injuries against the victims of crime, a "special relationship" is created when a person obtains an order of protection.[19] These court-issued orders were first introduced in 1976 to prohibit batterers from further contact with their victims. They encompass rather broad areas of jurisdiction, including evicting men from their residences.[20] There is controversy over the effectiveness of court orders in deterring violence against women, and some in the battered women's movement see them as merely a "piece of paper." Yet, the court found that such orders were, in fact, "an affirmative state commitment to protect the woman from her husband's harassment" (*New York Times*, 25 August 1988).

The threat of having a costly law suit brought against a municipality or police department increased during the 1980s. As a consequence, numerous localities adopted measures to enhance their responsiveness to battered women. Police departments instituted pro-arrest policies, maintained more thorough reports, and increased the availability and enforcement of protective orders.

---

19. For the purpose of this discussion, I have chosen not to formally distinguish between orders of protection, restraining orders, and no-contact orders, all of which serve the same basic end. Orders of protection are issued in a freestanding proceeding to restrain violence; restraining orders may be obtained in pending divorce cases; and no-contact orders are issued in pending criminal proceedings or are part of a sentence following conviction.

20. A majority of states have legislation explicitly permitting the eviction of batterers from their own homes. The 1986 Illinois Domestic Violence Law, for example, explicitly states that even when a batterer can claim a legal right to possession of his residence, the court must exclude him if the risk of his future abuse interferes with the petitioner's safe and peaceful occupancy (Epstein 1987, 7). Although this and similar laws have been challenged, they have been upheld, without exception.

Efforts were made to elevate both prosecution and conviction rates. By 1985, thirty-three state legislatures adopted pro-arrest policies for woman batterers while forty-seven of the nation's cities and six states specifically mandated them. Statutory changes in eighteen states also expanded police responsibilities by requiring officers to provide women with information about their legal options and services (Ferraro 1989, 157–160).

Additional events gained national attention and helped to inspire these reforms. Among these was the release of a 1984 study concerning arrest, funded by the National Institute of Justice and conducted within the Minneapolis Police Department. The study confirmed the assertions of battered women's advocates who argued that arrest was the most appropriate and effective form of police intervention in inhibiting violence against women. Police officers were given one of three strategies when responding to domestic emergency calls: (1) arrest, (2) counseling, or (3) sending the men away from the home for several hours. After analyzing more than three hundred cases, the researchers reported, "Arrest was the most effective of the three standard methods ... in deterring future violence" (Sherman and Berk 1984).[21] Further research modified this finding. Current research suggests that arrest is more likely to deter further violence among those offenders who are middle-class, employed, and white (Becker, Bowman, and Torrey 1994, 549). This suggests that arrest policies work best against those men who have enough privilege, thus respectability, to lose. Still, the Minneapolis study received considerable media attention and remains among the best known studies concerning police response.

The Attorney General's Task Force on Family Violence subsequently released a report recommending that "the chief of every law enforcement agency should establish arrest as the preferred response in cases of family violence" (1984, 22). In addition, the task force suggested that more judges be accessible on a twenty-four-hour basis to issue orders of protection and requested that every woman's complaint against her assailant be initiated by prosecutors on behalf of the state.

Several cities have since developed "victimless prosecution" policies for women too intimidated to pursue charges against their assailants. Cases may be prosecuted with evidence gleaned from

---

21. A follow-up study of biweekly phone calls with the same battered women and an examination of police records showed that after six months the percentage of repeated abuse was 10 percent in cases where police made arrests, 19 percent when counseling was used, and 24 percent when the man was sent away (Sherman and Berk 1984).

witness reports, emergency phone calls, photographs, medical reports, and other physical evidence. Approximately 60 percent of all cases prosecuted in San Diego involve this approach (*Ms.* 1994, 49). Similar steps have been taken by prosecutors in Philadelphia, San Francisco, Tulsa, and other cities (*Ms.* 1994, 49).

Victim/witness assistance programs and special prosecution units have been established in more than three hundred prosecutors' offices throughout the United States to more rigorously pursue men who batter. In many jurisdictions, judges are available around the clock to render decisions concerning orders of protection.

The results of these reforms have been impressive. Within five years after adopting a pro-arrest policy, for example, the police department of Rye, New York (population 18,000), reported that incidents of woman battery declined by 30 percent (Schmitt 1989). Furthermore, former New York Police Commissioner Benjamin Ward asserts that a pro-arrest policy is the most effective method of dealing with woman battery. From 1984 to 1988, arrests for battery have more than quadrupled in New York City, while the number of emergency calls received by the police increased only 5 percent.[22] Ward states, "Every arrest sends a clear message that violence in the home is just as criminal as violence in the streets" (Bohlen 1988).

The establishment of special prosecution units and advocates for battered women have been equally impressive. For example, since activists in Duluth, Minnesota, established the Domestic Abuse Intervention Project (DAIP) to coordinate the response of the criminal justice system, "81 percent of the women who use it are living in a violence-free situation within two years" (*Ms.* 1994, 35).[23] In Seattle and New York, conviction rates significantly increased after special programs were instituted (Lerman 1986).[24] Orders of protection have become easier to obtain and have been more rigorously enforced. Although many note that a man determined to harm a

22. A similar increase in the number of arrests has also occurred in Los Angeles (Bohlen 1988).
23. Established in 1980, this project was the first in the nation to coordinate the response of the criminal justice system. In Duluth, Minnesota, police follow a mandatory arrest policy, prosecutors and judges receive educational training concerning the seriousness of woman battery, and judges are given recommended sentencing policies ranging from thirty to sixty days for a first offense and harsher penalties for repeat offenses (*Ms.* 1994, 35).
24. For more data on these units and others, see Lerman 1986. She focuses on thirteen states that adopted reforms to reduce case attrition and obtain high conviction rates.

woman is unlikely to desist merely because a judge ordered him to refrain, orders generally have been effective in reducing abuse in cases involving less violent assailants; they should not be abandoned (Grau, Fagan, and Wexler 1984).

Feminists are acutely aware that reforms are no solution to woman battery, however. Indeed, they caution that more punitive policies may serve conservative ends. For example, they may exaggerate the protection the state affords women.[25] American feminists thus emphasize that reforms such as arrest and protection orders answer only to women's most immediate need for protection, and much remains to be done (Ferraro 1989).

Although the reforms described above have been generally satisfactory to those within the battered women's movement who demanded them (Ferraro 1993), there have been some troubling setbacks. For example, in several places maintaining mandated arrest policies, police began to arrest both the batterer and his victim. Such actions often stemmed from officers' resentment that the discretion they previously exercised when choosing not to arrest was challenged by new laws favoring and/or mandating it. Except for those rare occasions when battered women are technically culpable for harming men other than in self-defense, mutual arrest violates the liberty of abused women and discourages them from seeking police assistance in the future.[26]

Despite an increase in the number of referrals for prosecution, the number of prosecutions remains low and the indifference of many judges persists. To counter such insensitivity and enhance the accountability of judges to battered women, women's advocates submitted bills to various state legislatures that mandated educational programs for judges (*New York Times*, 3 May 1987).

Much less has been done at the national level. The federal government long asserted that the problem of women battery is primarily a responsibility that rests with state and local authorities. Activists, however, were generally pleased when the Congress and the Clinton administration changed this trend through the passage

---

25. This occurred in Sweden. In 1992, the new conservative government provided funding for bodyguards and safety alarms for battered women, while failing to adopt measures to more rigorously pursue their assailants.

26. Feminists responded to mutual arrests by drafting amendments to mandatory arrest laws. Frequently, these amendments explicitly state that only primary physical aggressors are to be arrested. In addition to clarifying police responsibilities, women's advocates recommended class action or individual lawsuits that claim damages and injunctive relief from false arrest. These actions have been useful in maintaining the original intent of pro-arrest policies.

of the 1994 Crime Bill, which contained provisions from the Violence Against Women Act (VAWA). Until recent discussions concerning this act, Congress had only twice before considered legislation concerning battered women; both times it was dismissed (Gelb 1983). Even the National Hate Crimes Statistics Act of 1990, which mandated the monitoring of hate crimes nationally, excluded crimes against women.[27]

Only under the Child Abuse and Treatment Act of 1984, which focused primarily on children, was direct federal funding previously allocated to specifically support shelter programs. That same year, President Reagan's Attorney General released a report on "family violence." While many commended the report for exposing the enormity of the problem, for supporting the work of shelters, and for favoring arrest and state prosecution, feminists criticized it on two grounds. First, it was gender-neutral: the report grouped all victims of domestic violence together and referred to woman battery as "spouse abuse" so as to avoid any political analysis that would require condemning woman battery as male violence. Second, activists noted, no funding was attached to the implementation of any of the recommendations (*SANEnews*, February 1986). The task force, instead, insisted that financial incentives be provided by the states to support shelters, conduct awareness campaigns, and train criminal justice personnel.

Senator Joseph Biden introduced the VAWA in June 1990 to reverse the lack of federal responsibility for this issue. After years of struggle, most of the key provisions of this act were incorporated into President Clinton's Crime Bill. To date, this is the most comprehensive federal legislation to combat violence against women. It authorized $1.6 billion to fund projects for abused women and improve the response of the criminal justice system over three years. "As a condition for receiving certain funds, states with particularly egregious domestic violence laws would have to show a stronger commitment to arresting and prosecuting domestic violence offenders" (Hirshman 1994). The act specifically allotted $325 million for

---

27. The National Coalition Against Domestic Violence and the National Organization for Women sought to rectify this exclusion through a series of meetings with the Coalition Against Hate Crimes, the group that sponsored the bill. With the conspicuous absence of any women's groups, the coalition consists of an otherwise broad spectrum of male civil rights, religious, and gay and ethnic rights groups, including world organizations such as Amnesty International. Member organizations unanimously agreed that they would not support a bill that included gender-specific violence. For a thorough analysis of why the Hate Crimes Act should explicitly include crimes against women, see Pendo (1994).

battered women's shelters and $3 million for a toll-free national hotline to provide women with critical information. It also created federal penalties for batterers who cross state lines in search of women fleeing from them.

The federal legislation not only provides much needed funding and important changes in criminal law but provides women with a civil remedy for the harms men commit against them. Women will be able to seek "compensatory and punitive damages through federal courts" if they can demonstrate that their abuser was "motivated—at least in part—by animus towards the victim's gender." As Linda Hirshman notes, "VAWA implicitly acknowledges that most violence against women is not gender-neutral, thus establishing that it is indeed motivated by gender-animus and is therefore a proper subject for a civil rights action" (1994, 46). This federal act essentially recognized woman battery as a hate crime in a way that the National Hate Crimes Statistics Act of 1990 did not.

Many within the battered women's movement were elated by the passage of this legislation. After all, they had struggled for a number of years to have it passed. Nonetheless, feminists remain aware that the proper implementation of this and other laws requires persistent oversight. Without such oversight, laws are poorly enforced and the monies that VAWA makes available may go into ineffective projects, particularly those that are least supportive of feminist goals.

The Swedish Case

Swedish women, like their American counterparts, attempted to enhance the responsiveness of the criminal justice system to battered women through legislative reform. In Sweden, as in the United States, the construction and adoption of laws involves an elaborate process. Activists cautiously pursued Sweden's few reforms for battered women.

Sweden's first reform was prompted by shelter activists who convinced the cabinet, political parties, and media that the existing rules of prosecution were inadequate (Duvander 1983). Rather than establish a new commission to investigate a change in the rules for prosecuting women batterers, the government conferred this task upon an existing committee, the Committee on Sexual Crimes.[28]

The committee offered its suggestion for reform in December 1981; the request that violence within the home be subject to public

28. This committee will be discussed further in the next chapter.

prosecution originally came from the women's organizations of the Liberal and Center parties. The new law was adopted in 1982, two years after it was originally proposed as a motion. It was not difficult to pass, as it required no additional expenditures and did not mandate arrest or prosecution.

Prior to this reform, the stated intent of Swedish legislators was to "protect the family and the sanctity of private life" (Dahlberg 1989, 225). The 1982 reform formally challenged this intent, as it enabled a third party to file a formal complaint against a batterer and allowed the victim to be absent from pleading against him in court. In addition, it enabled police officers to investigate and detain batterers, which they previously could not do unless the woman herself reported her assailant and requested prosecutorial assistance. By declaring woman battery a public offense, this reform expanded the possibilities for police and prosecutorial intervention.

Much like American pro-arrest reforms, this first reform acknowledged the reluctance of battered women to report their assailants and provided others with greater flexibility in pursuing criminal action. Unlike many American reforms, however, it did not specifically mandate the intervention of public authorities. Under the 1982 law, a prosecutor may assert that he or she, not the woman, is to blame for pressing charges; the implementation of the reform, however, depends entirely on the discretion and ability of the prosecutor to use it. Nonetheless, battered women advocates generally have been pleased with the recognition of battery as a public offense.[29]

Unlike the United States, Sweden has not established special prosecutorial units and/or full-time victim advocates. Since Sweden's prosecutors have overwhelming case loads and often lack the time, knowledge, and skills required to effectively handle cases of woman battery, activists requested legal aids. These individuals would provide services similar to those performed by American prosecutors and victim-assistance advocates.

The government formed a committee to investigate the request for legal aides for battered and sexually abused women. The committee

---

29. While there are no studies concerning the implementation and effect of this particular reform, Swedish authorities attribute the recent escalation in reported assaults to it. This, however, is unlikely, given that a study showed that most battered women lacked a general familiarity with the criminal justice system and that many did not even realize that their assailants had committed a crime (BRÅ, PM 1989:2, 32). It is, therefore, perhaps more realistic to attribute the increase in reported incidents of woman battery to the general acceleration of interest and heightened consciousness pertaining to battery that began in the early 1980s.

recommended that funds be allocated for raped women, but only under special circumstances for battered women.[30] It claimed that the cost of offering aid to all battered women would be prohibitive (SOU 1986:49). In response to protest from the women's sections of the political parties, the government reconsidered (Ingvardsson, interview, 1989). The Riksdag then passed a law requesting "greater generosity" for those special cases (Regeringens prop. 1989/1990: 158). Yet aid for battered women is still not mandated and courts determine eligibility on a case-by-case basis.

While the Swedish state adopted a reform relieving battered women of the responsibility for filing charges, thus enhancing cooperation and increasing the possibilities for successful prosecution, no special prosecutorial units or procedures were established, and legal aides were provided only under special circumstances. Women's advocates, though appreciative of the steps that were taken, noted that without greater commitment by the state, the 1982 reform will fail (ROKS 1990 Annual Conference).

Reformers eventually turned their attention from the successful prosecution of batterers to their victims' more immediate need for police intervention and protection. Since their establishment, women's shelters have had to deal with women who, after leaving their abusers, were further terrorized by them. In fact, after Stockholm's All Women's House was vandalized its board closed the shelter for a period of several months until it was convinced that it could provide adequate protection.[31] Several other shelters had experienced similar security problems. As a result, the national organization decided that securing protection orders for women would be an organizational priority.

Since many of the women involved in the battered women's movement are also active in party politics, it is not surprising that orders of protection were first proposed in 1986 by the Communist party (now the Left Party) and the women's sections of the Social Democratic, Moderate, and Center parties. The Riksdag then adopted orders of protection two years later.

No formal committee was established to investigate restraining orders. Numerous government officials attribute this to the speed with which the former Minister of Justice, Anna-Greta Leijon, requested action. The battered women's advocates clearly benefited

30. The term "special circumstances" remains nebulous. The provision of legal aid for raped women will be examined in Chapter 4.
31. The shelter was again vandalized in 1993 on New Years Day but this time remained open.

from the sympathy of this minister, who circumvented the usual formation of a formal investigatory committee. She simply had the bill written and immediately sent the draft out for comment. This led to the Riksdag's adoption of orders of protection, twelve years after their initial use in the United States.

This second Swedish reform makes it illegal for a man to contact a woman who has obtained an order (*besöksförbud*)[32] against him. It enables police to request that a man placed under an order leave the woman's premises immediately and/or cease to harass her. Prior to the adoption of such orders, police officers were unable to take any action against a batterer until he again harmed his victim. Under orders of protection, batterers' mere contact with or presence near the women they abused constitutes an offense punishable by up to one year in jail.[33]

Women must appeal directly to the prosecutor to obtain an order. Women's advocates object to this, saying that it sets battery laws back to their pre-1982 status. The women's section of the Center Party notes that if battering is to be considered a public offense, the law should give others, and not only the woman in danger of assault, the right to request an order of protection. Some prosecutors agree; they observe that charging women with this responsibility places them in danger of reprisals (Lynberg, interview, 1988; Qwist, interview, 1988). In addition, prosecutorial discretion remains a controversial aspect of this reform, especially given that so few women have contact with prosecutors.[34]

One year after the law took effect, the government appointed a police chief to conduct a brief study on the effectiveness of the orders.[35] The study found that 38 percent of requests for protection were denied (BRÅ, PM 1989:2). Prosecutors' reluctance to grant orders may be attributed to the wording of the reform, which explicitly discourages their use. The law states that "conflicts"

---

32. The literal translation is "visiting prohibition."

33. Originally, the punishment for violation was six months. The conservative opposition called for an increase, and, over the initial objections of the Minister of Justice, this request was met (SFS 1989:1075). Though not entirely displeased with the change, activists suspect that prosecutors may be more apprehensive about issuing orders of protection because the penalty for obstructing such orders is more severe (Kram, interview, 1993).

34. Other objections are contained in Swedish government records called "remiss" (Ds Ju 1987:13).

35. Only prosecutors and some shelter workers were surveyed. Since battered women were not, it is not known if they find the procedures to obtain orders complex and alienating, or if these orders deterred further assaults.

between men and women "should be solved in another way than through a restraint" and that orders are to be issued only under circumstances "where the general *threat* of punishment is not enough" (SFS 1988:688). Therefore, prosecutors have reserved orders primarily for men with prior criminal records.[36]

Protection orders are simply not utilized in those cases where American researchers found they might have the greatest effect. Similarly, the author of the government report concluded, orders have little effect on individuals with criminal histories who have shown that they are immune to punishment (BRÅ, PM 1989: 2, 38).

Women's advocates insist that the cautionary tone of the law be changed. They object to the condition that only men who have criminal records are eligible to receive an order. In addition, the shelter movement objects to the fact that, unlike American orders, Swedish orders may not be used to exclude men from the residences they share with their victims. Women who live with their assailants thus remain disqualified from seeking the protection prosecutorial orders could afford. To date, none of these concerns has been addressed by Swedish authorities.

Although orders of protection were intended to facilitate police intervention, the government found that "the possibility of police intervention in situations [the woman] experiences as threatening or frightening is very small" (BRÅ, PM 1989:2, 39). With more reason than in the United States, activists question the effectiveness of orders in deterring violence against women.

Eager to portray itself as a champion of women's concerns, though reluctant to directly confront the issues raised by activists, the conservative government took office in 1991 and increased funding for the provision of security alarms and similar equipment to women repeatedly subjected to physical threats. In some cases, women may even qualify for bodyguards.[37] Such action appears impressive. But, rather than limiting the mobility of men (through, for example, mandatory arrest policies), these measures restrict women's by making them reliant on security systems and bodyguards. Sweden's leading scholar on violence against women, Eva

36. More than 86 percent of the men who received them have prior criminal records, often involving prison sentences (BRÅ, PM 1989:2).
37. The securities industry stands to benefit from this expenditure. Indeed, one manufacturer of mobile telephones called ROKS to express disappointment that more phones were not being ordered by police for women's protection (Kram, interview, 1993).

Lundgren, argues that male dominance has been concretized by this paternalistic approach (1992a, 131).

Ironically, it was precisely the adoption of these controversial reforms that provided the government with ammunition for its recent assertion that "efforts to prevent various forms of violence against women have high priority in Sweden" (Swedish Institute 1993).

The current interest in violence against women resulted largely from the public's concern regarding violence more generally. The death of a boy in a street brawl, coupled with other street violence and property destruction throughout Stockholm and neighboring cities, prompted Social Democrat Prime Minister Carlsson to call an emergency cabinet meeting in 1989. There he proposed an investigation of violence in Sweden. ROKS was neither invited nor informed of the meeting, yet one shelter worker was in attendance. ROKS was angered both by its exclusion and by the fact that no similar action was deemed necessary despite the death of a woman killed nearly every week by male violence. The organization sent a letter of protest to the Minister of Equality, then Margot Wallström. In response, the minister requested that a separate committee on violence against women be formed. The government honored this request. The committee's directives provide a startling example of how the Swedish state regards sexual equality and violence against women:

> A society where power is not equally divided between the sexes can create a notion in men about power over women. This can produce a destructive consequence in that women are subject to a sexualized oppression, in the form of assault and degradation. (Civildepartementet 1989)

Women's sexualized oppression was, thus, attributed to an unequal division of power, an assumption later echoed in the final report (SOU 1990:92, 68).

That the government chose to attribute sexualized violence exclusively to the unequal division of power displays faulty reasoning. Although power is not equally divided among men, men are rarely subjected to sexualized oppression. The term sexualized oppression refers specifically to ways in which women are violated that men are not, or that are exceptional when they happen to men.[38] That these gender-specific violations are often sexual suggests also that they are

---

38. When men are abused, the perpetrators of that abuse are almost always other men. Women do not use sexuality to assert gender dominance; "women who engage in vulgar, abusive behavior are scorned, not empowered by the male responses they

frequently arousing for the men who perpetrate them.[39] It is precisely one's ability to find sex-specific violations "sexy" that numbs one's capacity to object to, and be outraged by them. The government failed to consider that women's inequality in the labor market, or anywhere else, may be attributed to sexualized oppression or that sexual equality is impossible to promote in states where women's sexualized oppression remains unacknowledged. Indeed, the Swedish government moved to suppress this kind of assessment when the Minister of Justice insisted on the dismissal of the committee's first secretary, Märit Röger.

In the report for which she was later fired as committee secretary, Röger discussed the pervasiveness of sexualized violence in Sweden and its centrality to other forms of women's oppression. Her report was subsequently edited and released as an informal working paper (Civildepartementet 1991). Contrary to her findings, the paper attributed violence against women to factors such as alcohol, drugs, and alienation—not sexuality. It made few connections with the desire batterers have to control and sexually use women or their more general contempt for them. In addition, the working paper constantly referred to the government's formally published report on general violence despite the fact that the report contained only a cursory mention of woman battery (SOU 1990: 92). In this manner, the government could maintain that it covets sexual equality without exposing itself as unable to promote it effectively. Eventually, however, this tactic proved insufficient.

The Social Democratic government's numerous shortcomings were successfully exploited by the bourgeois coalition that replaced them in 1991 (Elman 1993). The following year, reported instances of assault increased by 10 percent. Stating that such a significant increase "can hardly be attributable only to increased tendencies to report such crimes" (Directive 1993:88, 5), the new government, like its predecessor, called for the establishment of a special investigatory commission on violence against women. The commission's

---

get" (Langelan 1993, 54). By contrast, men assert their sexuality to ensure their dominance. This is, in part, what is meant by sexual oppression. Sexual oppression, sexual abuse and violence against women are inextricably interwoven. Sexual domination is both rooted in and furthered by oppression that is sexualized, and this includes the violence that men commit daily against women.

39. These violations, as earlier suggested, include, but are not restricted to, rape, sexual harassment, prostitution, woman battery, and femicide. The sexual appeal of these crimes has been noted by feminists within Sweden (Lundgren 1992b) and the United States (MacKinnon 1987; 1989; 1994).

findings were recently released under a Social Democratic administration that regained power in 1994 (SOU 1995:60). The commission's report contains several suggestions designed to better provide support to abused women. For example, in recognizing the failure of gender-neutral statistics to accurately reflect the incidence of woman abuse, the commission echoed earlier requests that gendered crime statistics be maintained. The commission also recognized that Sweden's social service agencies and the criminal justice system lack the awareness and expertise necessary to effectively serve abused women (SOU 1995:60). Yet, the commission entrusted these same ineffectual authorities to develop internal progress reports, training and educational programs. Despite the obvious expertise of shelter activists, their role in monitoring or providing educational support to these agencies was not emphasized. Rather, shelters are to continue to provide direct, "practical" assistance to battered women and are to receive additional funding for this purpose. The commission also suggested increased spending for men's crisis clinics and other organizations that provide treatment to perpetrators.

The commission revealed a disquieting incomprehension of law. In stating that "legislation alone cannot solve the societal problems posed by violence against women," the commission failed to recognize that the importance of law is less in solving the problems that stem from violence against women than in promoting a firm opposition to its occurrence by criminalizing such abuse (SOU 1995:60, 433). Nonetheless, the commission proposed revising the criminal code to outlaw those behaviors which "effectively contribute to establishing a situation characterized by mental terrorization" (SOU 1995: 60, 444). Under this reform, it remains unclear which acts of terror would be prohibited that are not already criminalized. Police intervention was not mandated to ensure compliance with this reform or those the government adopted previously.

Those expecting significant change from this recent commission report are likely to be disappointed. One of the most important functions commissions provide is that they make activists who want change think that something is taking place that will allow for it to occur. One of Sweden's leading political scholars, Olof Ruin, notes that such reports are "utilised for much more than a direct basis for concrete measures"; they are "used as a legitimating device, as a substitute for action" (1982, 161). Märit Röger concurs. Reflecting upon the previous investigation, she suggested that it was established to supplant any direct action that was originally requested by shelter activists through their national association. For example, at the time of the first report, ROKS had requested the greater availability and enforcement of protection orders. After five years and several government reports, little has been done to insure their implementation or availability. The most recent investigation resembles previous ones in that it underscores the need for further studies. Röger maintains that Sweden is slow to act and that it is "a very repressive society when it comes to matters like power, sexuality and violence" (letter to author, 21 January 1991).[40]

Summary

From its inception, the battered women's movement in Sweden, unlike its American counterpart, channeled its demands through the traditional political system. Indeed, given the centralized structure of the state, it had little choice. The Social Democrats, for example, could and did determine the structure of one of the first shelters for battered women (i.e., the All Women's House) against the wishes of feminists who for years had worked to obtain the site for all women, not only those who had been battered. Moreover, many early shelter activists were (and many still are) active in the women's sections of Sweden's political parties. Thus, the few suggestions for legislative reforms that were made were proposed through the parties. Moreover, they were drafted by ministerial bureaucrats who, unlike most authors of American model laws, had no knowledge of the specific obstacles faced by battered women in the criminal justice system.[41] Lastly, the monitoring of reforms is the preserve of the state, through government-appointed commissions, bureaucrats, or ombudsman. By contrast, the American battered women's movement often relies on lawyers, researchers, and others not affiliated with the state.

The absence of a relatively autonomous means of initiating, monitoring, and appealing reforms in Sweden has not concerned most scholars who, like Adams and Winston, argue that "the persistent

---

40. After Märit Röger was released from her duties as committee secretary, she was directed by her former superior to remain silent concerning the details of her dismissal. She was then assigned to another post within the ministry and has kindly granted me permission to discuss what happened to her.

41. This may explain why reforms were less extensive in Sweden than in the United States, where, for example, orders provide protection for women who share their residence with men.

effort to involve bureaucratic agencies in policy formulation helps to ensure their cooperation in implementation" (1980, 12). However, an inventory and assessment of laws and services available to battered women in Sweden leads to a somewhat discouraging view of corporatist policy formation.

Compared to the United States, the Swedish state has taken less interest in violence against women. Reforms are far fewer and less comprehensive and date only from 1982. In addition, while reforms in the United States often mandated particular programs for battered women or the responsiveness of public authorities to them, Sweden's reforms remained discretionary. No action has ever been mandated. In Sweden, as in the United States, reform efforts focused on legislation to enhance prosecution and provide women with greater protection against further abuse. In the United States, however, these efforts led to an increased interest in police intervention at the state and local level. In Sweden attention centered on prosecutorial powers, and reforms were adopted at the national level by the Riksdag.

The lack of local initiatives in the development and implementation of reforms for battered women is standard within Sweden's centralized corporatist state. The fact that social reforms are almost always adopted at the national level could have been positive, in that, once a reform favorable to women is adopted, the entire country must abide by it. Yet, like the United States, the national level of the Swedish state was generally impermeable to women's gender-specific requests. While the national level of the United States was also reluctant to act on the requests of women, its federalist structure permitted and even encouraged the development of more innovative policies and programs for women at the local level. Eventually these local efforts furnished a platform from which activists would succeed in making grander demands on the federal government—demands that materialized in the adoption of the 1994 Violence Against Women Act.

 4

STATE INTERVENTION AND RAPE

Rape is fundamentally an act that manifests, sustains, and promotes a systematic context of women's subjection.[1] Like woman battery, rape is a gendered act that is almost universally committed by males and overwhelmingly directed against females. Although incarcerated males and young boys are also victimized, the vulnerability to rape that "girls share with boys—age—dissipates with time" while, "the vulnerability [that] girls share with women—gender—does not" (MacKinnon 1989, 176).[2]

Both the fear of rape and its actual occurrence permeate women's lives.[3] Catharine A. MacKinnon notes that "rape and the fear of rape operate cross-culturally as a mechanism of terror to control women" (1991, 1302). Swedish feminists express similar sentiments. Maria-Pia Boëthius, author of Sweden's first feminist book on rape (1976), insists that for women rape is the greatest violation.

As Susan Griffin notes, the mere threat of rape diminishes women's presence in the world (1986). When the rapist is a family member, for example, women sometimes leave their homes. When the threat is the fear of the unknown rapist, women remain locked inside. When outside the home, the fear of rape limits their mobility (Rich 1979, 242). In addition, women's financial independence is further compromised by the precautions they take against rape. These may, for example, preclude job opportunities or require

---

1. Throughout this book, the term "rape" is broadly employed to refer to forced, manipulated, or coerced sexual activity.
2. Because this book focuses on the state's response to women's demands, I have chosen to limit my discussion of rape to adult women only. Consequently, I will not be addressing the sexual abuse of girls.
3. For example, a study of perceptions of violent crimes among residents of Seattle, Washington, reported that all women fear rape. Most report that to them it is more terrifying than any other crime, including murder, assault, and robbery (U.S. Department of Justice 1987).

Although no similar research has been done in Sweden with specific regard to rape, a government study found that nearly two of three women stated that they refrained from going out at night for fear of being violated (Edqvist and Wennberg 1983, 319).

numerous investments in cabs, safer locks, well-lit homes and neighborhoods, self-defense classes, and unpublished telephone numbers. Finally, rape may end in murder. Men do kill women after and sometimes even before they sexually abuse them (Caputi 1987; Radford and Russell 1992). And, while venereal disease and pregnancy have always concerned rape survivors, women are now worried about contracting the deadly HIV virus from their rapists. Recent efforts to confront the AIDS epidemic have, however, focused on the importance of practicing "safer" sex without acknowledging that this is a meaningless concept for women who are forced to have sex.

Despite the fact that most women are raped by men they know,[4] both Swedes and Americans generally believe that "real" rape involves a violent attack by a stranger (Estrich 1987; SOU 1994:56, 13). When rape does not conform to this conception, it is unlikely that a woman will be able to perceive herself, or be perceived by others, as having been seriously violated. Consequently, in both countries, rapes are under-reported, making empirical evidence difficult to obtain. In addition, the legacy of racist law enforcement in the United States has been an additional deterrent for women of color to report rape.[5] Black women, in particular, are "less likely to report their rapes, less likely to have their cases come to trial, less likely to have their trials result in convictions and, most disturbing, less likely to seek counseling and other support services" (Collins 1993, 101). As Patricia Hill Collins, a professor of Afro-American studies, writes: "Far too many African American women live with the untenable position of putting up with abusive Black men in defense of an elusive Black unity" (1993, 102).

While it is hard for women to reveal that they have been battered, Diana E. H. Russell insists that "more women appear to have been willing to disclose violence in marriage than forced sex" (1982, 38). Prior to Russell's study of rape in marriage (1982), documentation of wife (and girlfriend) rape was obtained mostly through studies of woman battery. When battered women in the United States were specifically asked if they were also "pressured to

---

4. In the United States, studies show that rape by acquaintances, including boyfriends and husbands, is more common than rape by strangers (*Response* 1984, 9). In Sweden, a recent investigation found that almost half of all recent reported incidents involved rapists whom the women knew (BRÅ, PM 1989:2).

5. Swedish law enforcement practices are also suggestive of racism; studies show that immigrants get into trouble with the law twice as often as Swedes and are overrepresented among those charged with crimes (BRÅ 1983:4).

have sex" by their batterers, 73 percent of the 137 respondents answered affirmatively (Frieze 1980). In a study of eighty-two battered women in Sweden, 76 percent responded yes to a similar question (Elman and Eduards 1991).[6]

While these studies illuminate the existence of coerced sex, they leave unchallenged the idea that rape is merely another form of abuse suffered only or primarily by battered women. Russell warns that:

> although ongoing intimate heterosexual relationships that are violent often involve both rape and beating, it is also important to recognize that the issues of rape and wife beating can be quite separate in many marriages, and that wife rape is not merely one more abuse suffered by the already battered woman. (1982, 21)

Some men batter women but do not rape them; some men rape women but do not batter them; and others do both.

One reason many wish to conceive of rape simply as another form of violence is precisely because, as Catharine MacKinnon writes:

> The point of defining rape as "violence not sex" or "violence against women" has been to separate sexuality from gender in order to affirm sex (heterosexuality) while rejecting violence (rape). The problem is what it has always been: telling the difference. The convergence of sexuality with violence, long used at law to deny the reality of women's violation, is recognized by rape survivors, with a difference: Where the legal system has seen the intercourse in rape, victims see the rape in intercourse.... Instead of asking, What is the violation of rape, what if we ask, What is the non-violation of intercourse? To tell what is wrong with rape, explain what is right about sex. (1983, 646–647)

MacKinnon notes the difficulties women have in articulating what is wrong with rape because it frequently resembles intercourse. One might wonder if MacKinnon has entertained the possibility that women may have as much trouble explaining "what is right about sex" as they have had in asserting what is wrong about rape.[7]

---

6. We asked the women if they were "forced to have sex." The major problem in determining the extent of marital rape is in the subjective viewpoints of the respondents. Many women are reluctant to describe any coerced sexual experience with their husband/ex-husband or boyfriend/ex-boyfriend as rape. Objectively, what occurred to them may fit any of a number of definitions of rape. In our study, we consciously decided to couch the question in the less threatening term, "forced sex." As of this writing, this study is the only survey research concerning woman battery and rape in Sweden.

7. For a thought-provoking feminist critique of sexuality, see "Sex Resistance in Heterosexual Arrangements" by A Southern Women's Writing Collective (1990).

Michel Foucault insightfully noted that sex becomes what it is socially understood to be (1978). It took years for (radical) feminists to fully appreciate this. For example, when feminists objected to battery, pornography, rape, incest, prostitution, genital mutilation, sadism, and masochism, they were often caricatured as "anti-sex." Stunned, they retorted that it was not sex itself that they opposed but rather the various abuses of it. That response clearly demonstrated their initial failure to comprehend that the abuses to which they objected constitute sex as it is "socially" experienced and understood. In other words, what is clearly abusive for feminists is experienced by many (usually men) as merely sex and, therefore, not violative.[8]

Despite his reputed brilliance, Foucault had a significant shortcoming. His insistence that sexuality is what it is socially perceived to be fails to explain why, for example, a feminist understanding of sexuality is rarely socially understood. Like many intellectuals, Foucault had a gender-neutral view of social construction that obscures rather than illuminates who it is that has the power to construct social reality.[9] That women are part of the social whole does not mean that women are equally complicit in the erection of social constructs. Women, *as a group*, do not have the luxury of determining what sex is and how they do or do not want to have it, because, within the context of male dominance, women are often regarded simply as "sex" (Elman 1993b).[10]

All women experience the effects of rape. Even if they are never actually assaulted, every woman is a potential victim. The fact that women constitute 97 percent of all sex crime victims in the United States suggests that male victims exist but are exceptional (Pendo

---

8. Catharine A. MacKinnon writes: "Most rapists ... continue to live in society undetected or unpunished and unrehabilitated. *In many instances, one must suppose that they remain unaware that they did anything even potentially culpable*" (1991, 1303, my emphasis).

9. The view that sexuality is "socially constructed" is certainly preferable to DNA destiny (i.e., biological fundamentalism), but this does not mean that it should be readily embraced. I am reluctant to support the notion of "social construction" when it conceals the gendered dimensions of political reality and absolves men from their responsibility for specific actions that are injurious to women and other men.

10. It is precisely because women have been made into sex that in arguing against prostitution one is said to be against the women in it. This is particularly fascinating; a similar logic is absent from discussions of other oppressive conditions. For example, critics of capitalism are not easily subjected to charges of being against workers, and abolitionists are not said to be racist. To favor prostitution is to support the sexual enslavement of the women in it. Consequently, women are not regarded as fully human but as the sex that the system of prostitution extracts from them (Elman 1993b).

1994, 165). Comparable statistics within Sweden do not exist because the state fails to use gender as a category of record for either the perpetrators or victims of sexual abuse.[11] Nonetheless, the state has consistently recognized that women constitute an overwhelming majority of those raped, while the perpetrators are almost exclusively men (Directive 1993:88; SOU 1994:56; SOU 1995:60). Even when the victims are male, the perpetrators are other men, not women. Rape is, thus, a man's act.

Women are targeted for sexual abuse. In fact, studies of convicted rapists indicate that women are chosen because they belong to the class "women":

> [Women are regarded as] collectively responsible for the rapists' problems. In some cases, victims were substitutes for significant women against whom the men desired to take revenge. In other cases, victims were thought to represent all women, and rape was used to punish, humiliate, and "put them in their place." In both cases women were seen as a class, a category, not as individuals. (Scully and Marolla 1993, 42)

Similarly, an investigation conducted by the Federal Bureau of Investigation that found that 95 percent of serial rapists reported choosing their victims on the basis of gender (in Becker, Bowman, and Torrey 1994, 232).

Because rape has such a disparate effect on women, as women, policies and programs developed within this area clearly reveal the commitment and capacities of each state in responding to women's concerns.

The United States

Consciousness, Crisis Centers, and Other Support Services

The American movement against rape, like that against battery, was linked to the larger feminist movement. Many early anti-rape

---

11. This fact has raised eyebrows, as Sweden is a country known for its conscientious maintenance of statistics on everything from the average weight of Swedes and levels of skin cancer to political attitudes (Elman 1991, 39). Moreover, authorities have long maintained data on the ethnicity of both the perpetrators and victims of sex crimes. They also differentiate between those rapes committed outdoors and rapes committed indoors, although there is no record of whether the perpetrator is known to the victim.

In 1995, the Commission on Violence Against Women has suggested that statistics be maintained to reflect the gendered dimension of rape (SOU 1995:60).

activists emerged from the feminist consciousness-raising groups, which provided them with an understanding of rape as a collective female experience. In fact, the first anti-rape demonstration and conference was organized by the New York Radical Feminists (NYRF), a group that wished to combine consciousness-raising with theory and action (Hole and Levine 1971, 152–157).

On January 24, 1971, NYRF held a "Speak-Out on Rape." It was the first time American women gathered publicly to disclose their sexual abuse. The speak-out was an important step toward redefining rape in ways that challenged the prevailing myth that women desire and/or enjoy being raped. The rally also established testimony upon which further action and analysis was possible. Four months later, NYRF organized a conference against rape. Speakers described their assailants and analyzed traditionally held political, social, and psychological assumptions concerning rape. NYRF published the conference papers and additional information in *Rape: The First Sourcebook For Women* (Connell and Wilson 1974).

Many of the early anti-rape activists had, themselves, been raped. They understood rape from both a personal and a broad social perspective. This understanding was quintessential in establishing an agenda that included peer support to sexually assaulted women and the improvement of public services. For example, activists insisted on competent medical staff who could both collect evidence of rape from pelvic exams and provide immediate detection and protection against pregnancy and venereal disease. Activists also proposed rape prevention activities such as self-defense courses, neighborhood safety patrols, and public information campaigns.

The most direct and often the first services feminists provided were twenty-four-hour telephone hot-lines and crisis-companion services through which trained volunteers met women immediately following their sexual assault. Meetings typically took place in hospitals, at police stations, and sometimes in courts. Volunteers offered women immediate legal advice and crisis counseling and provided referrals to gynecologists, psychologists, support groups, lawyers, and others.

These low-cost, path-breaking services were relatively easy to establish and relied entirely on private funding and extensive volunteer networks. These services usually began in large cities; the Rape Crisis Center in Washington, D.C., was the country's first. Formed in 1972, the center served as a prototype for subsequent services by disseminating information through its handbook, "How to Form a Rape Crisis Center."

Within three years, anti-rape activists had established rape crisis lines and groups (often called WAR groups, Women Against Rape) in nearly every major city and college community.[12] In addition, the National Organization for Women (NOW) developed approximately two hundred rape task forces throughout the United States, including one at the national level (Center for Women and Policy Studies 1975). By 1976, there were approximately four hundred centers, and by 1979 the number of rape-related services reached one thousand (Largen 1981).

Although the rape crisis centers of the early 1970s usually developed independently of each other, their striking similarities may be attributed to the pervasiveness of the feminist movement from which they grew (Rose 1977; *Victimology* 1976). There are now nearly one thousand rape prevention educational programs on college and university campuses alone, compared with one in 1972 (Celis 1991). The continued growth of this movement makes it impossible to provide exact figures on the number of all centers and services operating today.

Like battered women's advocates, those originally working against rape consciously opposed all hierarchy. Policy-making within most centers was decentralized, and the traditional professional-client relationship was supplanted by peer counseling. The absence of paid staff was an explicit "rejection of the idea that women who have been sexually assaulted need professional help" (Pittman, Burt, and Gornick 1984, 1). Volunteer involvement was, however, not simply an outgrowth of feminist ideology; it was imperative. Rape crisis centers lacked the money with which to establish paid positions.

Centers that were unable to support themselves through private sources merged with other organizations, such as hospitals or established women's centers. Feminist activism and analysis was often marginalized as some "parent" agencies imposed conventional structures that prevented the collective work feminists hoped to accomplish. Many centers, however, did benefit from a degree of institutionalization. They were stabilized and could coordinate activities that were "previously left to chance communications among harried volunteers" (O'Sullivan 1978, 51). This improved the quality and increased the number of services that the staff could offer. In turn, more raped women requested their assistance.

---

12. For details on the establishment of these groups, see Grimstad and Rennie (1973, 145–159).

In 1973, a quickly overburdened rape crisis movement requested funding directly from the federal government. NOW's Legislative Office and National Rape Task Force Coordinator worked closely with U.S. Senator Charles Mathias to adopt legislation. Once passed, it funded rape crisis centers and authorized a national study concerning the effectiveness of state rape laws and public agencies in their treatment of victims. The bill also established a clearinghouse, the National Center for the Prevention of Rape, to compile continuing studies, conduct research, and promote training programs for police officers and medical personnel. Although pleased by these developments, feminists were concerned that the training programs would supplant or coopt existing centers. In addition, some activists were skeptical of the government's emphasis on research as opposed to action (*Victimology* 1976).

In 1974, the Law Enforcement Assistance Administration (LEAA) completed its first study of rape. LEAA found that responses to rape cases by police, hospitals, and prosecutors were overwhelmingly "poor," "inadequate," and "haphazard." LEAA made recommendations that were nearly identical to those made by feminists. They called for the development of local programs and procedures that would provide better treatment for raped women (Brodyaga et al. 1975). Hospitals added rape crisis services. Police departments recruited women to act as community liaisons and pursue rape investigations. Prosecutors' offices formed special rape units.

The relationships that many centers had with their communities began to change. Reforms in state agency structures and services encouraged a once skeptical anti-rape movement toward greater cooperation with police departments, prosecutors, and social services. In addition, many women who previously would have contacted centers for assistance were being served within public agencies instead. Early rape crisis centers were therefore relieved of the large numbers of women who often taxed their small volunteer staffs. However, these same centers were slowly denied their claim to knowledge and expertise.

Within a decade, all-volunteer, nonprofessional, collective rape crisis centers became anachronisms. While volunteers still constitute a majority of the staff, most rape crisis centers now have some hierarchical structure with paid staff and professional counselors (Pittman, Burt, and Gornick 1984).

The transformation of feminist crisis centers into relatively professional service organizations can be traced to a variety of interrelated factors. Perhaps the most important factor was that as the anti-rape movement grew, it was increasingly able to make demands on the state. Through highly visible activities such as speakouts and "Take Back the Night" marches, the movement gained considerable media coverage and exposed many of the most abusive conditions to which state agencies, like social services and police departments, subjected women. In response, almost every state adopted reforms that required its agencies to adopt some rape-specific protocol (Bienen 1983). In addition, state and local governments provided economic support to crisis services.

The state, in turn, made its requests. Centers applying for state support were forced to make organizational changes in order to fulfill highly competitive funding requirements for government grants. Such changes required, for example, that centers hire educated professionals and incorporate boards of directors. As more professionals became involved in anti-rape work, nonprofessionals increasingly deferred to them. The state was promoting "a relatively conservative, social service approach to this issue" (Matthews 1993, 177). For this reason, many centers refused to apply for government funding. They maintained only minimal, low-cost, volunteer services and/or applied for private funding (Gornick, Burt, and Pittman 1983, 4–8).

State support was clearly an agent of professionalization. Some feminists emphasize the mental-health professions' sudden interest in rape as a clinical, rather than a political, issue (Friedman 1981). Yet again, one may attribute this interest to the availability of state resources. Regardless, the state's involvement contributed to a climate in which meeting the needs of sexual abuse survivors became less alien. Many centers and specialized units within public or private professional institutions such as hospitals were established, employing professional personnel with government monies. In Los Angeles, for example, the impetus to establish services for raped women came "from Black community organizations responding to the state's call for proposals" (Matthews 1993, 179). An unanticipated consequence of state funding was that it "furthered one of the more progressive goals of the U.S. anti-rape movement: to become multiracial and multicultural and to expand services to all women" (Matthews 1993, 177).[13]

---

13. In 1978, Angela Davis wrote: "If Black women are conspicuously absent from the ranks of the anti-rape movement today, it is, in large part, their way of protesting the movement's posture of indifference toward the frame-up rape charge as an incitement to racist aggression" (in Collins 1993, 101). Collins notes that such

The current position of rape crisis centers on the use of professionals varies. The more radically inclined centers are operated predominantly by volunteers who insist that some women might need professional counseling but most do not. They assert that having professional staff is contrary to their message that rape can and does happen to any woman and that women are best assisted by their peers. Centers that emphasize professionalism assert that peer counseling is insufficient. Most centers, however, agree that long-standing "nonprofessionals" acquire such expertise that they frequently become a center's greatest asset (Pittman, Burt, and Gornick 1984). Furthermore, over time, professionals who came into rape crisis work from outside of the feminist movement began to regard themselves as feminists (Matthews 1993).

Despite problems associated with over-work, professionalism, and occasional public hostility, the major achievement of the anti-rape movement has been the centers it created (Rose 1977). This accomplishment should not be underestimated. A national survey of rape crisis centers concludes:

> All over the country many staff in police, hospital, prosecutor, and mental health agencies are acting on premises of respect for victims and rejection of the more destructive rape myths. Public and private funding supports rape crisis centers that were non-existent ten years ago. And professionals of all types recognize some responsibility to know about reactions to rape and to treat victims decently. (Burt, Gornick, and Pittman 1984, 17–18)

Although the movement's accomplishments are impressive, others insist that the more radical demands of activists have been adjusted to a "liberal, service oriented norm." Many now involved in fighting against rape do not "espouse the premises on which the anti-rape movement was founded" (Burt, Gornick, and Pittman 1984, 18). Critics argue that state intervention and professionalization undermine the feminist goal that women, themselves, must regain control of their lives (Scott and Dickens 1988). Additionally, they note the erasure of the fact that rape is an act of misogyny—a crime of men against women.

---

absence also "fosters Black women's silence concerning a troubling issue: The fact that most Black women are raped by Black men" (1993, 101).

Sweden

Authoritative Discourse and Few Rape Crisis Services

In Sweden, the public discourse concerning rape originated from government-appointed commissions and not, as in the United States, from a context within which women could assert that they, themselves, had been raped. Because of their general skepticism of feminist analysis and the absence of an autonomous feminist movement, Swedes acquire most of their knowledge about rape from bureaucrats and state-employed researchers, not from feminist activists.[14]

In 1971 the Social Democratic Minister of Justice, Lennart Geijer, appointed a commission to investigate sex crimes. This initiative resulted neither from feminist lobbying nor from a desire to mitigate sexual assault. Rather, the commission was informed by the sexual libertarianism of the 1960s, a period in which "the sexual exploitation of women was becoming more and more pervasive" and "sexual freedom became ... a commercialized commodity" (Wistrand 1981, 72). The commission's agenda proved consistent with these values.

In 1976, Geijer's Committee on Sexual Crimes released its final report (SOU 1976:9). Committee members called for a "modern perspective" regarding sexual assault. For them, this meant that rape should be considered a "minor crime," because, they argued, a woman's behavior is contributory. Consequently, the Social Democratic committee insisted that the scale of penalties for those found guilty of sexual assault be made milder (SOU 1976:9, 21). Additionally, they proposed that "the present provisions on incest, which are directed against sexual relations with offspring and siblings, be abolished" (SOU 1976:9, 23).

The report met with such protest from the women's sections of the political parties that none of its recommendations was adopted. Although protests are exceptionally rare in Sweden, outrage over the recommendations overcame even the traditional distaste for dissent.[15] A year later, the Social Democrats lost control of their government and consequently this issue. They were replaced by the

---

14. Indeed, the leading public authority on rape is a male criminologist, Leif Persson. Maria-Pia Boëthius, a feminist writer, was spuriously labeled a fascist by a book reviewer in Sweden's largest daily newspaper, *Dagens Nyheter* (Ekselius 1990). This charge was based simply on the fact that she views rape as central to patriarchy.

15. It is also worth noting that this protest was more acceptable because women could claim their concern rested more with the fate of children than with themselves and others as women.

first nonsocialist government coalition to hold power since the early 1930's.[16] Sven Romanus, an independent parliament member, succeeded Geijer as the Minister of Justice. Calling Geijer's committee "invalid," Romanus immediately established a new commission. Its purpose was to "intensify the reaction of society to the serious assault that rape implies" (SOU 1982:61, 23).

In 1977, the nonsocialist government established Sweden's first (and only) rape clinic, in Stockholm. The clinic met women by appointment only and operated within the government's association for sex education (RFSU). Its primary function was therapeutic. The women who organized the clinic, Eva Hedlund and Maria Granö, rejected the notion that rape is a "woman's issue" and sought a "more integrated and professional response" to sexual assault (interview, 1988).[17] Unlike the feminist founders of the American anti-rape movement, they clearly saw themselves as professional service providers and viewed the women who came to them both as clients and as objects for study. Indeed, the clinic was established not merely to provide counseling but to equip the new commission with information that could be used to initiate proposals that would better meet the needs of sexual assault victims.

In 1982, the commission released a report that explicitly rejected the analysis and proposals of its predecessor. It was unwilling to consider a woman as an accomplice to her own rape. A woman's prior sexual behavior, therefore, was to have no bearing on a rape case. The commission also opposed the sexual abuse of children both in and outside of the family (SOU 1982:61). It suggested that the criminal justice system and medical institutions be better equipped, through information and training, to meet the needs of raped women and called for them to establish more efficient routines

16. While the left, or more specifically the Social Democrats, is frequently credited by non-Swedes with policies beneficial to women (Norris 1987; Verba 1987), it is vital to note that most equality policies were adopted between 1976 and 1982. During this period a nonsocialist coalition held power. The Social Democrats supported many of the most progressive policies and commissions initiated by their bourgeois opposition only after these steps were initiated. This will be discussed in Chapter 5. For work specifically relating to the Social Democrats as an unreliable feminist ally, see Elman (1993a).

17. At the time of the interview, Maria Granö was in charge of educational outreach for RFSU. Eva Hedlund serves RFSU as both a therapist and consultant. Hedlund also served on the governmental commission concerning legal aid for battered and raped women. When asked where they had obtained their expertise, they replied, "We went to the United States to learn from you." They studied with therapists, not with those working in grass-roots crisis centers.

to obtain evidence for prosecution. Yet, as with woman battery, no specific guidelines or training was offered or mandated.[18]

The Social Democrats regained power the same year the commission released its report. The Social Democrats took no initiatives to develop other centers, crisis lines, or alternatives that would have specifically addressed the recommendations made by the prior bourgeois government. This inaction reveals that the party is not a trusted promoter of women's issues as so often suggested in the literature (Elman 1993a). In fact, their newly formed government eliminated funding to the rape clinic, and, as a result, it closed. RFSU therapists still counsel some raped women, but on an informal basis. Battered women's shelters continue to provide emotional support and legal advice to sexually assaulted women.

In 1988, a series of critical newspaper articles focused on the criminal justice system's poor handling of reported rapes. Journalists noted that reported incidents had increased 73 percent, from 769 in 1975 to 1,332 cases in 1988. At the same time, however, the number of cases ending in conviction significantly decreased. In 1976, nearly all rape cases (98 percent) ended in conviction. Ten years later only one-third of such cases were successfully prosecuted (Agebjörn and Hellman 1988).

These articles prompted the Social Democratic Minister of Justice to call for an immediate internal investigation to determine whether the increase in reported rapes was "illusory" or "real." In other words, were more rapes occurring or were more women willing to report that they had been raped? Although investigators conceded, even within the report, that the proposed research question was impossible to answer definitively, their analysis produced a conclusion that pleased the government.

The government-appointed investigators insisted that the journalists provided an "erroneous interpretation of statistics" (Ds 1990:3, 78). They then provided an explanation for the 73 percent increase:

> We conclude that the increase in reported rapes during the reported period can essentially be attributed to the substantial increase in the category of rapes committed indoors. (Ds 1990:3, 37)

---

18. Even those now conducting criminal investigations are self-taught. For example, Per-Olov Forslund, who once headed investigations of sex crimes in Stockholm, explained that his own expertise resulted from having read a special guide on "Family Violence" (Forslund, interview, 1988). Nonetheless, he is currently responsible for the implementation of educational programs for social service and criminal justice personnel throughout Sweden (Forslund, interview, 1993).

Within this category of "indoor rapes" they found that "the suspect is already known [to the woman] when the report is filed." With this in mind, the investigators reasoned that the "statistics do not show any general increase in the crime of rape" (Ds 1990:3, 37). According to this logic, the increase in reported rapes was "illusory" because rapes committed indoors by known assailants could not be seriously considered as "real." This clearly reflects the inability of Swedish authorities to give credence to the complaints of women raped by men they know. Given the government's position, it is surprising that women in Sweden would report these violations at all.

The government then utilized the report to launch a defense against its critics and to allay the fears of Swedish women. The Riksdag magazine declared that "the mass media had made a total mistake when stating that rape had become more common" (Från Riksdag & Departement, 1990:8, 7). The report was essentially a public relations exercise to justify the Social Democratic government's diffidence in taking more specific action in combatting the crime. In focusing on whether the increase in reported rapes was "real," the government diverted the media's attention away from the incompetence of its authorities. In consequence, the many women who had come forward were ignored.

More recently, when the National Council for Crime Prevention and the Bureau of Statistics confirmed a 25 percent increase in sexual offenses reported between 1991 and 1992, the newly elected conservative government assumed a more responsive posture than its Social Democratic predecessor. It declined to consider the increase as illusory. Instead, under the direction of Minister of Social Affairs Bengt Westerberg, it appointed an investigatory commission and directed it to examine "the underlying causes and mechanisms of violence" (Directive 1993:88, 13). In addition, this Commission on Violence Against Women had the task of proposing recommendations to improve the support and services available to sexually abused women. In its interim report, it asserted the need for a single, government-sponsored center for raped and battered women (SOU 1994:56). With the final report now complete (SOU 1995: 60), preliminary steps are being taken to establish a crisis center within Uppsala University Hospital under the directorship of a physician. It will provide direct care to abused women on a twenty-four-hour basis, conduct training for health-care professionals, and serve as a national resource center. Given the recent release of this report and the promise of future work, it is too soon to determine if these developments will lead to any significant changes in the treatment of raped women. While the commission's objective has been to suggest ways to better meet the needs of abused women, researchers from the National Council for Crime Prevention have focused on the "ethnic underclass" the Council feels is responsible for the problem. Rape is increasingly portrayed by Swedish authorities and the press as a "foreign" problem. A recent newspaper article reports the Council's recent finding that 60 percent of rapists in Stockholm are either of foreign descent or are Swedish men born abroad (Fälth 1994). This is particularly significant when one considers that immigrants constitute less than 10 percent of the population. Possible reasons for the notable overrepresentation of foreign men were not discussed.[19] In an age of alarming increases in xenophobia (Ministry of Foreign Affairs 1991), the notion that rape is a "foreign" problem strikes a responsive public chord.

In Sweden, it is difficult to think of any other crime that has elicited as much sympathy for, or interest in the motives of, the perpetrator.[20] A year after the RFSU rape clinic closed, Eva Hedlund released a study entitled *Rape—Powerlessness: 60 Men Tell Their Stories*. The "purpose of the book was to understand rape from the rapist's perspective" (Hedlund and Lundmark 1983:1, 11). Lacking a feminist analysis (i.e., failing to recognize that men hold power over women), the authors consider rapists to be powerless. They regard rape as an unfortunate mishap for "both parties." In an article about three therapists working with men convicted of rape, a writer for one of Sweden's largest daily newspapers, *Svenska Dagbladet*, proclaimed that the rapist is a "confused child" (Nilén 1986). Like Hedlund, the therapists strenuously referred to the rapist as a victim.

Public discourse concerning rape has consistently favored a therapeutic approach to a more punitive one (Lundgren 1992b). Even

---

19. For example, reporting rates may be higher for inter-ethnic rape because Swedish women may perceive that they are more likely to be believed in such cases. The possibility that Swedish authorities rebuff reports pertaining to Swedish men and more vigorously pursue foreign men was not examined. In the United States, the criminal justice system has furthered racism by disproportionately targeting African American men for public probes and punishment. It is not impossible that this is happening in Sweden.

20. While some research has already been done on rapists (Hedlund and Lundmark 1983:1), there remains a dearth of original research on raped women in Sweden. Consequently, a feminist criminologist insists that Swedish authorities depend on victim studies conducted in the United States and Great Britain (Leander, interview, 1988).

Maria-Pia Boëthius, one of Sweden's most renowned feminists, prefers "centers for restoring men's dignity" to prison. Within such centers men could "relearn their sex roles" (1976, 122–123). Therapy for rapists, however, has been disastrously ineffective in Sweden. Professor of psychiatry Sten Levander conducted a study of 177 Swedish sex offenders and found that those sentenced to special psychiatric care programs showed high levels of recidivism.[21] Levander insists that the Swedish state follow Norway's example and place only psychotic rapists under psychiatric care. Rapists, he argues, are criminals.

In the absence of a formidable, autonomous feminist movement, the state established Sweden's only rape clinic. State-appointed bureaucrats readily claimed an expertise that they then utilized to oppose those who argued that the state had abandoned its responsibilities to raped women. In their 1990 investigation of rape, they skillfully defended the government against its critics by confining the debate to a statistical accounting of reported incidents of rape. Their current emphasis on "foreign" rapists serves to reinforce the presumption that rape is a recent import. To date there has been no original Swedish research on raped women that transcends these parameters. A centralized, state-sponsored rape clinic in Uppsala University Hospital is unlikely to alter this because it is to be firmly established within the confines of the state and under the directorship of a physician, not an activist.

In both Sweden and the United States, state intervention was an agent of professionalization. Yet, in Sweden, with few resources external to the centralized state's reach and no alternatives to either state-financed programs or commission work (Heclo and Madsen 1987), women were unable to counter this professional emphasis. Even the founders of the first Swedish rape clinic, though well-intentioned, approached raped women from a paternalistic viewpoint rather than from a feminist viewpoint that deemphasizes the notion that raped women are clients: a clinical rather than political designation. In contrast to their American counterparts, they refused to identify with the women they counseled. In fact, the founders even resisted the notion that rape was a woman's issue.

21. Of the 177 offenders who committed their crimes between 1971–1975, Levander found that after fifteen years, 73 percent of those committed to psychiatric care repeated their offense. He notes that before his study it was assumed that the level of recidivism was only 10 percent. Another frightening finding was that 10 percent of these men later committed murder (Lindahl 1990).

Unlike American women, Swedish women were confident that the state could provide services for raped women. Only later did many find themselves mistaken. In Sweden, not surprisingly, responsibility for practical assistance to sexually assaulted women fell to the already overburdened battered women's movement.

The Criminal Justice Systems: Common Obstacles

While definitions of rape vary slightly among different American states, rape in the United States, as in Sweden, is generally defined as forced sex with accomplished penile penetration (however slight) and the absence of consent. However, women in both countries have obtained a more expansive definition of rape allowing them to prosecute other forms of sexual abuse, not just those involving heterosexual intercourse.[22] But, because so few cases are tried and because even fewer result in convictions, feminist attorneys, like Leigh Bienen, note that changing the definition of rape "can never have more than a marginal practical effect" (1983, 134).

While legal definitions of rape are remarkably similar in Sweden and the United States, comparable data on incidents, arrests, prosecutions, convictions, and punishments are virtually impossible to provide.[23] Because comparative statistics are often unreliable, our focus generally will remain on the capacity of the states to recognize and respond to injustices within the criminal justice system.

Rape, unlike woman beating, has always been considered a criminal act. Thus, the problem of American and Swedish women has

22. Both states have also defined rape in gender-neutral terms to enable the prosecution of men who rape other men. Yet, broadening the definition of rape in this way essentially ignores the gender-specificity of the crime. The most recent Commission on Violence Against Women in Sweden proposed a consideration of linguistic changes in the law to remedy this (1995: 60, 279).
23. Despite this, Gilbert Geis noted that Swedish and American rates of rape per 100,000 inhabitants are remarkably similar. He did his research in the 1970s, a time when activists in each country had begun their reform efforts. He found that the reported rape rate in Stockholm was 21 per 100,000. In Minneapolis, an American city heavily populated by those of Swedish descent, the rate of reported incidents was 20.5. In New York the rate was 22.3 and in Boston 12.8 (Geis 1978, note 96). More recent cross-national comparisons are very difficult because, since the 1970s, there have been an increasing number of subtle differences between these countries with regard to how the crime is defined and how statistics are compiled. Although the Geis data is old, one should appreciate that it dates from a time during which women began their rape reform efforts.

been less in having rape, itself, regarded as criminal than in having specific cases regarded as coercive enough to warrant public outrage, credulity, and legal redress.

In both states, raped women and their advocates depict individuals within the criminal justice system as slow, abrasive, indifferent, and incredulous. Recent national statistics found that Swedish police considered approximately 30 percent of all reported incidents to be "unfounded" (Leander 1992, 8), compared to 15 to 20 percent in the United States (Tong 1984, 101). "Unfounded" are those cases that police do not pursue. These cases often result from an unwarranted police skepticism towards rape complainants and a low probability of conviction.[24] Prosecutors, like police, exercise tremendous discretion and are not required to explain their reasons for dismissing a case. Both have also been characterized as hesitant to provide women with legal redress (Estrich 1987; Gustafsson 1989; SOU 1995:60).[25]

Given a woman's reluctance to report rape and the police and prosecutor's willingness to drop cases, few claims ever reach court. Once in court, a woman's victimization does not end, but recommences with a vengeance as defense lawyers insist the woman either misidentified the assailant or welcomed the sex. Despite reforms, defense lawyers often focus on a woman's sexual history to weaken her credibility. They insist that if a woman previously consented to sex with the accused, she likely did so again. By contrast, in both countries, even a man's record of previous convictions for sexual assault is inadmissible.

In the United States for many years, a woman's credibility was further compromised by judges who issued "cautionary instructions" advising juries to regard a woman's testimony skeptically. A standard version of this instruction reads:

---

24. They can also result from, among other things, a women's unwillingness to cooperate with a police investigation.
25. In Stockholm, raped women can wait as long as six months for the police to investigate their cases (Malmborg 1989). This compromises the ability of the police to pursue meaningful investigations. As a consequence, they drop many cases for lack of sufficient evidence. After a woman said she was raped in an elevator in Stockholm's Central Train Station, police told reporters that the rape did not occur because their week-long investigation failed to uncover a suspect or any witnesses (Brännström 1990). American police officers similarly approach raped women with suspicion. The New York City Police Department, for example, deprived a woman police officer of her gun and badge after she reported that a fellow officer raped her. The accused male police officer was similarly deprived of his gun and badge. *Both* officers are currently under investigation (*New York Times*, 10 April 1991).

A charge such as that made against the defendant in this case, is one which is easily made and, once made, difficult to defend against, even if the person accused is innocent. Therefore, the law requires that you examine the testimony of the female person with caution. (Tong 1984, 105)

Over the last few decades, this practice has been abolished. While Swedish judges have no history of such instructions and do not issue them now, the nation's Supreme Court cautioned that it must be proven "beyond all doubts" that a man is guilty of rape if he is to be convicted (Högsta Domstolens 1980:137). No similar caution was issued for any other crime.

Within both legal systems men may be convicted of rape only if prosecutors can prove that the accused was both aware of the woman's dissent and disregarded it.[26] Raped women in both countries are typically expected to demonstrate the absence of their consent through physical resistance. In the United States, this is *de facto* if not *de jure*. Law Professor Deborah Rhode notes that this requirement reflects the sexist "death-before-dishonor philosophy" (1989, 247). This doctrine was recently exemplified when a grand jury refused to indict a rapist who was convinced by his victim to wear a condom. One juror stated, "... some jurors believed that the woman's act of self protection [against HIV] might have implied consent" (Milloy 1992, 30). No other offense requires victims to "risk intensifying their injuries in order to prove them" (Rhode 1989, 247).

In response to the significant bias against them, raped women and their advocates sought legislative and administrative reforms to improve their treatment within the criminal justice system and increase the likelihood of successful prosecution. The remainder of this chapter examines the specific efforts of women within both states, their successes, and their shortcomings.

The American Case

The anti-rape movement has been less litigious than the battered women's movement because, for raped women, the goal has been less to have laws properly enforced than to have them reformed.

---

26. This intent requirement, however, has been abandoned in a number of recent American cases. The Maine Supreme Judicial Court, for example, declared in *State v. Reed* (1984) that rape "requires no culpable state of mind." And, Pennsylvania's Superior Court held in *Commonwealth v. Williams* (1982) that "even a reasonable belief as to the victim's consent would not exculpate a defendant charged with rape" (in Estrich 1987, 94).

Traditional rape law provides women little redress even as it affords men vast protection against accusation.

Rape law has conventionally operated under the assumption that women lie. Seventeenth century British jurist Sir Matthew Hale instructed juries that rape is an accusation "easily to be made and hard to be proved, and harder to be defended by the party accused, tho' never so innocent" (Estrich 1987, 5). Later, nineteenth century behavioral scientists, such as Sigmund Freud (1969), added scientific credibility to Hale's instruction. Courts came to believe that sexually repressed women seduced innocent men and, to save their reputations, later declared they had been raped. This logic provided the foundation upon which judges issued "cautionary instructions" (Brownmiller 1976, 434).

To guard against the complaints of immoral, guilt-ridden, and spiteful women, American law added uniquely stringent rules of evidence to safeguard men from false accusation. Courts established "corroboration requirements" which meant that a woman's assertion of rape had to be supported by other evidence, such as physical bruising, torn clothing, or a witness. In no other criminal proceeding is the jury advised to take special care in evaluating a victim's testimony. Only in a rape trial is the adversary presentation of evidence deemed so insufficient that corroborative evidence is necessary. Anti-rape activists have also noted that, given the nature of rape, such evidence is extraordinarily difficult to obtain. There are rarely witnesses, for example, and even medical evidence may establish penetration but not absence of consent.

Given the evidentiary rules, rape is not an accusation easily made nor is a man's guilt easy to prove. Under these circumstances, the essential question for feminists is how to make rape trials equitable so that sexually assaulted women have some legal recourse.

The repeal of all cautionary instructions and corroboration requirements were among the first reform objectives of the anti-rape movement. In April 1971, New York Radical Feminists (NYRF) held a follow-up conference to their anti-rape "speak-out." This event helped launch intensive lobbying campaigns directed at the New York state legislature. Two years later, NYRF and other anti-rape groups organized, in coalition with law enforcement officials and civil liberties groups, a National Rape Prevention Month. They held workshops, lobbied national and state legislators, and raised media consciousness. Feminists thus gained the momentum necessary to secure reforms in New York as well as in other states.

Feminist activists convincingly argued that the requirement of corroboration reflected a sexist disbelief of a woman's word. The corroboration of a victim's testimony was not required for the conviction of any other crime. Research confirmed their assertion that "none of the justifications for treating rape cases differently from other criminal charges stands on solid empirical or theoretical footing" (*Yale Law Journal* 1972, 1390–1391). By 1974, only thirteen states had not completely abandoned the requirement of corroboration (Rose 1977, 79). Activists used these same arguments to successfully advocate the banning of cautionary instructions.

Feminists experienced similar victories against the introduction of a woman's sexual history in court proceedings. They noted that this information was one of the primary obstacles to a woman's ability to persevere throughout a rape trial, and that, furthermore, its admissibility unfairly placed the woman, not the man, on trial. By 1983, more than forty state legislatures passed "rape shield" laws that restrict, if not totally exclude, evidence concerning the woman's prior sexual conduct (Bienen 1983).[27] The 1994 adoption of President Clinton's Crime Bill extended rape shield laws to all federal criminal cases. Some defense attorneys, however, concede that, despite these reforms, they are able to introduce testimony about a woman's sexual past. In fact, a majority of defense attorneys who were interviewed after extensive reforms had been passed in Michigan admitted that they still actively solicit this information about the victim (Marsh, Giest, and Caplan 1982, 55).

While rape shield laws have not revolutionized the legal stance of women, they have helped decrease the importance that those within the criminal justice system attach to the victim's past (Estrich 1987; Stanko 1985). This change in attitudes cannot be solely attributed to these legal reforms, however.

Legal reform was but one component of the anti-rape efforts made to enhance the criminal justice system's responsiveness to the demands of raped women and their advocates. Feminists worked alongside attorneys and operated within public agencies to improve counsel and services for sexually assaulted women. Through sustained educational efforts, they demanded specially trained police units to obtain and pursue sexual assault reports. They noted that this would improve the quality of evidence and ultimately increase the number of rape convictions. When criminal statistics supported

---

27. The only exceptions permitted under these restrictions are to allow evidence showing the source or origin of semen, pregnancy, or disease.

their claim,[28] police departments throughout the nation established special units (Rose 1977).

While the anti-rape movement successfully challenged evidentiary rules and helped institute special police procedures and units, such advances were irrelevant for the victims of rape in marriage. Traditional law provides explicit immunity to husbands by defining rape as "forced sexual intercourse with a female *not the wife* of the perpetrator." This "marital rape exemption" has its roots in English common law and the dictum of Sir Matthew Hale, who wrote "by their mutual matrimonial consent and contract the wife hath given up her self in this kind unto her husband which she cannot retract" (Estrich 1987, 72). Hale's "irrevocable consent" doctrine was readily incorporated into American law.[29]

The issue of rape in marriage did not receive national attention until 1978, when Greta Rideout unsuccessfully brought action against her husband in Oregon. The following year, feminists in Berkeley, California, founded the National Clearinghouse on Marital and Date Rape to monitor legislation and provide information to those interested in combatting rape in marriage and rape by acquaintances. Eventually the clearinghouse helped coordinate reform efforts throughout the United States.

Many legislators have been resistant to reform. California State Senator Bob Wilson stated, "If you can't rape your wife, who can you rape?" (Estrich 1987, 74). Others insisted that rape in marriage either is not serious or does not exist. The research of Diana E. H. Russell (1982), however, clarified that it is frightfully common and may be even more traumatic than rape by a stranger.

28. New York Women Against Rape, for example, convinced the city police department to establish a special sex crimes unit to be directed and staffed by women. Subsequent studies then showed that when women police officers pursued rape reports, significantly fewer cases were classified as false and unfounded. Previously, 15 percent of cases were classified as unfounded. Within less than three years, the rate was only 2 percent, a figure corresponding to the rate of false reports for other violent crimes (Brownmiller 1976, 435).

29. Two common law doctrines helped buttress Hale's dictum: the concept of marital unity, by which a husband and his wife are considered one person, and the view that women are chattel. A husband owned his wife's body as he did his own. Consequently, the legal profession reasoned that a man could not rape himself.

Women have been more successful in challenging legal restrictions on their rights to property than they have in establishing their right to sexual autonomy. By 1839, state legislatures had begun to adopt reforms that removed the most blatant restrictions on the rights of married white women to make contracts, hold property, and retain their earnings independently of their husbands. After the Civil War, similar rights were extended to black women (Rhode 1989).

Legislators argued that lifting exemptions would burden courts with complaints made by vindictive wives against innocent husbands. Scholars suggest, however, that accusations of rape are less easily made and proven than other serious criminal accusations. The stigma that accompanies women who assert violation keeps rape the most under-reported major felony (Estrich 1987, 10). Rape is distinguished from other crimes not because of the "disproportionate numbers of actual complaints but because of the disproportionate numbers of cases that are never reported" (Estrich 1987, 54).

While legislatures have been slow to address rape in marriage, courts have been more responsive (Rickenberg and Schulman 1984). Like battered women's activists, those fighting against rape invoked the Fourteenth Amendment. They persuasively argued that marital-rape exemptions were in direct violation of the equal protection clause (National Center on Women and Family Law 1988). By 1981, courts in Florida, Massachusetts, and New Jersey agreed and refused to grant husbands immunity from prosecution for rape. New York and Pennsylvania joined them in 1985 and 1986, respectively. These decisions helped to facilitate additional efforts to overturn other exemptions (National Center on Women and Family Law 1988). According to the National Coalition on Marital and Date Rape, as of November 1991, all but two states (North Carolina and Oklahoma) had removed the marital-rape exemptions (Becker, Bowman, and Torrey 1994, 241). At present, no state offers an explicit exemption, yet a majority of states present a confusing array of partial exemptions for husbands.[30]

The results of these reforms have been mixed. The director of the National Clearinghouse on Marital and Date Rape stresses that the conviction rate for husbands prosecuted for rape is 85 percent (X 1987, 1). The removal of marital-rape exemptions, however, appears to have had little practical effect on a wife's willingness to prosecute (Bienen 1983). Still, the exemption became a focus of reform "less because feminists believed that its erosion would result in widespread prosecution than because its presence remained symbolic and symptomatic of gender domination" (Rhode 1989, 250).

Although most evidentiary rules specific to rape have been repealed and marital-rape exemptions are far less frequent, "force has

---

30. States often require women to show they have taken steps to end their relationship. In Michigan, Indiana, Kentucky, and Tennessee, only legally separated wives can charge their husbands with rape (National Center on Women and Family Law 1988). The 1994 Crime Bill may inspire change in this area, however, because it requires that federal laws treat acquaintance rape and stranger rape the same.

replaced consent or corroboration or unchastity as the primary doctrinal rubric" for expressing the court's skepticism toward raped women (Estrich 1987, 57). This was, in part, one unintended consequence of the theory created by some feminists who wished to deflate issues of consent by "convincing courts in particular and society in general that rape is more a crime of violence than of sexual passion" (Tong 1984, 112).

Feminists initially favored an approach that deemphasized the sexual component of rape because it is more acceptable for women to object to violence than it is for them to say that they do not want sex. By assimilating rape in the category of assault, feminists also hoped to prosecute husbands who, while often immune from rape charges, could still be tried on assault charges.

Deemphasizing the sexual component of rape solves some problems while creating others. Estrich warns that incorporating rape under assault law would equate the failure to fight (and perhaps further risk a woman's life) with submission, which will be interpreted as consent (1987, 62). Similarly, it makes it almost impossible to punish a rapist unless he subjected the woman to substantial physical trauma. Many rape victims sustain no discernable physical injuries. "Most assaults occur through threats of force, and victims' most common response is verbal protest" (Rhode 1989, 247). Women do not fight like men; "they react like people who have already been beaten—or never had the power to fight back in the first place" (Estrich 1987, 62). Catharine A. MacKinnon (1989) and others maintain that rape is no less a violation if violence does not accompany the coerced sex. The victims of theft do not have to prove that they resisted in order to convince others they did not consent to having their money taken (Estrich 1987). Moreover, one would hardly argue that a theft has not occurred unless violence accompanies it.

Assimilating rape under assault law also lessens the penalties rapists are likely to receive. Some argue that a decrease in penalties inevitably benefits victims because juries are reluctant to convict men of rape if they feel the punishment (e.g., death, life imprisonment, twenty-five years) is disproportionate to the crime (Tong 1984). There has, however, been no conclusive evidence to either support or refute this position.

Those unsatisfied with the redress that criminal courts provide have turned increasingly to civil courts. Even if criminal charges are never filed or have been dismissed, victims may sue their perpetrator for civil damages. Rapists may be sued for personal injury such as the intentional infliction of emotional distress. One benefit in pursuing this route is that standards of proof are generally less strict for civil than for criminal cases.

In the past, raped women rarely considered this option. While criminal action is taken on behalf of "the people" (i.e., the state), civil suits are prosecuted on behalf of women by privately retained lawyers. Few of these rapists apprehended have the resources to make it worth a woman's efforts. In recent years, however, women have begun to sue not only their assailants but a variety of third parties, because the possibility of winning such civil suits has increased (Ehrhart and Sandler 1986). For example, colleges may be held responsible for inadequate security measures that contributed to a woman's abuse in her dormitory or elsewhere within the institution. Both to protect their reputations and to shield themselves from law suits, colleges (and other institutions) are developing rape prevention policies and programs.

The overall results of the American approaches and reforms examined here remain unclear. Some insist that most reforms are essentially inconsequential because they are not properly implemented for the benefit of women (Marsh, Giest, and Caplan 1982). More specifically, rape reforms do not appear to have increased convictions (Bart and O'Brien 1985, 129–131). Others implore us to appreciate the radical impact on public attitudes that has been achieved through these reforms. Even the symbolic value of these reforms should not be underestimated (Spohn and Horney 1992).

Legal reform served the critical function of politicizing rape as a crime while simultaneously focusing attention on women's sexual inequality. The state now recognizes the anti-rape movement as a politically effective force.

> Rape has achieved the status of a "serious problem" in the eyes of the Federal Government, law enforcement officials, mental health professionals, social science researchers, and others in positions of power and control. (McDonald 1976, 6)

With this change came a "new recognition that the state is not only responsible for controlling crime, but also for compensating its victims in order to remain legitimate" (Matthews 1994, 6). Accordingly, in 1994, Congress moved to mandate restitution for the victims of federal sex crimes and broadened the possibilities for civil prosecution. In addition, the federal government plans to provide additional funding for research to evaluate laws and examine ways to reduce crimes against women. Despite such activities at the federal level, most action still takes place at the local level.

Anti-rape activists remain keenly aware that the attitudes and commitments of those within the criminal justice system are vital in determining the effectiveness of reforms. For this reason, they have worked hard to convince the system to embrace their views. They have lobbied legislators and provided educational programs for judges, law enforcement personnel, and the general public. Their efforts have not been without result.

Today, the idea that the state should offer women protection and legal redress is commonly accepted. The state's "conception of harm caused [by rape] has undergone radical redefinition." There is also the "recognition of the fact that all women are at risk" (Bienen 1983, 149) and "it is now unusual to hear the view that rape or sexual abuse rarely occurs" (Bienen 1983, 148). With this in mind, the movement established a foundation of support services and reforms both within and outside of government institutions. For American women, legal reform was considered only one means, and the criminal justice system only one target. The movement's continued success depends on both its willingness and its ability to engage all levels of a decentralized state and society to achieve its goals.

The Swedish Case

According to traditional Swedish law, rape was a serious and harshly punished crime. Indeed, until 1779, the penalty for rape was death. But, the severity of this punishment did not reflect a concern for women's bodily integrity. Rather, the function of rape law and the severity of punishment reflected a desire to preserve and protect patrimonial property. Women were male chattel (Dahlberg 1989, 230).

As in the United States, rape was theft of sexual property belonging to a father and/or a husband. The fact that it was originally conceived as a property offense, and has socially and legally evolved within this framework, resulted in the legalization of rape in marriage until 1965 and the enduring legitimacy of coerced sex within other intimate relationships thereafter.

Unlike American law, however, Swedish law has been little influenced by British tradition. Women in Sweden were thus spared some of the explicit legal dictums derived from Hale. For example, within Sweden there are no formal "cautionary instructions" or "corroboration requirements." In practice, though, it is rare that a woman's assertion of sexual abuse is viewed without suspicion.

While Sweden lacks explicit corroboration requirements, it does maintain an express requirement of intent. Consequently, if a man believed, however wrongly, that a woman consented to sex, he cannot be convicted of rape. Prosecutors are, thus, burdened to prove, beyond doubt, that the accused knowingly disregarded a woman's nonconsent. This emphasis on the perpetrator's intent forces courts to consider consent from the man's perspective, and from this perspective consent is often inferred. Indeed, a Swedish court recently ruled that a mentally retarded woman was not raped because she could not dissent (Tagesson 1990).

In Sweden, as in the United States, nonconsent is usually determined through physical resistance. This effectively "immunizes those men whose victims are afraid enough, or intimidated enough, or frankly smart enough not to take the risk of resisting physically" (Estrich 1987, 96). Moreover, even when resistance is clear from the woman's perspective, it is rarely sufficient to establish the man's intent to rape. The infamous Malmö case provides an excellent example of this. The court freed two men, A and S, because the woman's resistance:

> may have been experienced by A and S as "becoming" and as the "conventional" resistance that takes place during the initial stages of sex. Therefore, the men did not take her resistance seriously.... Even if it can be said that A and S exercised some amount of violence during the initial stages of the sexual act, it cannot be said to have been sufficiently proven that they did this with the intention of forcing her into the act. (Dahlberg 1989, 217)

The court, thus, concluded that there existed considerable doubt that the two men raped the woman.

The Malmö case brought considerable protest from the women's sections of the parties, from the shelter movement, and from other women's organizations. They demanded that the Minister of Justice reprimand the court. The minister not only refused, he insisted the court responded appropriately. Boëthius argues that the minister's position encouraged the courts to operate, against women, "in compliance with their prejudices" (Boëthius 1989).

As a consequence of the courts operating "in compliance with their prejudices," only the most brutal rapes can be prosecuted successfully. Unless extreme levels of violence accompany the rape, it is even doubtful that the courts will consider a violation to have occurred. Prosecutors know this and are unwilling to pursue cases unless they can prove the woman "fought back," because, as

Prosecutor Qwist states, "with an absence of violence, rape is hard to prove." In other words, a woman's saying "no" is enough to establish neither her unwillingness to have sex nor the man's intent to force sex upon her. As Qwist frankly interprets the reality of the law, "we need more than just her words" (interview, 1988).

Attacking a woman's credibility is essential to a man's defense. In Sweden, as in the United States, this frequently is accomplished by probing into the woman's sexual past. In general, the belief that a woman's sexual past is related to her present assertions of sexual violation reflects the law's unwillingness to protect women who fail to meet its version of virtue. Thus, it is not surprising that when a prostitute recently insisted she had been raped, Stockholm's Court of Appeals ruled that prostitutes are unworthy of full redress (Stenius 1990). This emphasis on the claimant's character casts onus on the victim and weakens the prosecution's case. These factors make conviction even more unlikely, if not impossible.

In 1981, the women's section of the conservative Moderate Party pressured the party to propose that measures be taken to improve the position of women victims in court; however, they did not provide any specific recommendations on how to accomplish this goal (Motion 1981/1982:874). A year later, the Committee on Sexual Crimes acknowledged that a raped woman is

> subjected to insinuating and trying questions regarding her behavior and way of living, especially from the defendant's lawyer. It is said of such trials that they are often more stressful for the woman than the assault itself. (Boëthius 1989)

The committee concluded that this situation is "unworthy of a society founded on the rule of law" (Boëthius 1989). To remedy this, it recommended a reform that would explicitly prohibit courts from being influenced by a woman's sexual history.

By 1983, the Center Party united with the Moderates to support the committee's proposed reform (Motion 1982/1983:314). These two parties were then joined by the Liberal Party, which also suggested that legal aid be provided to raped and battered women (Motion 1982/1983:685).

This "bourgeois" coalition called for reforms to improve the legal redress courts provide raped women. The left did not. Instead, the Social Democrats suggested that additional money be provided for projects to rehabilitate those already convicted of rape. They wanted rapists to "receive a different and positive view of women" (Motion

1983/1984:2177). The Communist Party, during this period, remained silent on rape-related issues.

By July 1984, however, all parties in the Riksdag agreed to a law reform that would prohibit courts from regarding a woman's sexual history as relevant. In addition, the law permitted rape victims to have someone with them during legal proceedings as a source of social support. The women's sections of the political parties and the shelter movement wanted further steps taken to assist raped women. In response, the government instructed the Legal Aid Committee to investigate the possibility of extending legal aid to the victims of sexual abuse and violence (*Side by Side* 1985, 73–74).

The July 1984 reform was similar to the American rape shield laws that took effect years earlier. Yet, unlike rape shield laws, this Swedish reform did not expressly prohibit the introduction of a woman's sexual history. It only directed the court to disregard such material. As in the United States, the reform did provide women with some protection, but it did not completely eradicate the demeaning sexual insinuations of defense lawyers.

Bias against women pervades the legal system. The shortcomings of the 1984 reform in the face of such bias were acknowledged by the Legal Aid Committee, two years later, in its report on legal aid for the victims of sexual abuse and violence (SOU 1986:49). The report contended that the quickest and most effective way to resolve this issue would be to establish rape education programs and provide sexually assaulted women with legal aid. In 1988, two years later, the government allocated 250 million krowns ($42 million U.S.) for legal aid to sexually abused women. The funding, however, was limited to the payment of salaries to legal aides, whose only qualification for these positions is that they are lawyers (Lavén, interview, 1988).

Shelter activists were generally pleased that the government took action to improve the situation for raped women. They would have preferred, however, that the expenditure be spent on a broader range of victim services and educational programs rather than on legal aides who work with those few women who have the strength to enter court. Moreover, the duties of legal aides appear to replicate those already provided by prosecutors and others. Shelter volunteers, social workers, and friends who provide support to assaulted women in court, as well as outside of it, do so without recompense or for a nominal fee. Perhaps the most telling criticism of these reforms is that they have not increased conviction rates.

Despite the various shortcomings of Sweden's rape reforms, married women and women within similar relationships are not denied formal legal redress. As early as 1965, Sweden altered its statute so that husbands could be charged with raping their wives. This change stemmed from Riksdag debates and not from any specific feminist requests. Some members of parliament argued that "all persons" should be able "to determine for themselves whether they shall participate in sexual intercourse." Others insisted that abandoning the exemptions would result in burdensome accusations from vindictive women (Geis 1978, 297). The government sided with those who believed that women had the right to deny their husbands/lovers sexual access.

According to Gilbert Geis, the government's response to the marital-rape debate was "pragmatic: implement the principle ... because it is a just principle" (1978, 297). Simply stated, people should be free to determine if they want to have sex. Anita Dahlberg, a law professor and director of the Center for Research on Women at Stockholm University, has a somewhat different understanding of the circumstances underlying the adoption of the reform. She notes that the government did not specifically seek to abolish marital-rape exemptions but, rather, made only a semantic change. The change, she said, was initiated by legal experts who simply wished to have a more encompassing criminal code (interview, 1993).

While the government abolished marital exemptions, it established different penalty structures "for varying kinds of rape in order to alleviate any fear that husbands convicted of marital rape might be liable to ... draconian responses" (Geis 1978, 297). Strangers convicted of rape received prison terms of no less than two years and not more than ten years. By contrast, husbands were vulnerable to prosecution only for sexual assault, which carried a penalty of no more than four years in prison. Consequently, "Under Swedish law, a pre-established relationship automatically renders the defendant liable to a lesser sentence in a rape attack" (Geis 1978, 299).

The overall effect of this 1965 reform was first assessed eleven years later in the 1976 report on sexual crimes (SOU 1976:9). The committee conceded that "Reports to the police of rape in marriage and marriage-like cohabitation rarely lead to court proceedings" (SOU 1976:9, 9). In fact, by 1976, there had been only four reports of marital and cohabitation rape, none of which resulted in conviction (Geis 1978, 299). Some attribute this to the reluctance of women even to consider they had been raped. They note that Swedish women are expected to regard sexual encounters casually, including those that are abusive (Geis 1978). This cultural expectation, coupled with the insensitivity of criminal justice personnel, has deterred Swedish women from seeking legal redress. Others believe, however, that the fact that few instances are reported suggests that rape in marriage and marriage-like relationships is not a serious problem in Sweden.[31] This debate continues today.

After nearly twenty years, the law against marital rape was formally strengthened. The 1984 rape reform also stated that the relationship of the woman to her rapist was to make no difference. Yet this reform lacked specificity. As a result, even the different penalty structures for strangers versus known rapists were retained.

The Swedish experience with marital-rape reform is a persuasive reminder that the consequences of such reforms cause little or no mischief to either husbands or the criminal justice system (Geis 1978; Rhode 1989, 250). It is ironic that Sweden's most progressive rape reform, the 1965 amendment, is used by reformists elsewhere to appeal to the opponents of further reform by acknowledging the rather insignificant effect it has had.

Summary

In essence, Sweden's rape laws were less problematic than those of the United States, so fewer reforms were required to improve them. There were neither cautionary instructions nor explicit corroboration requirements to remove. However, in practice, given the intent requirement, Swedish women share the same burdens of proof that were legally encoded and still required of American women.

While Swedish laws were less overtly offensive, the criminal justice system continues to operate "in compliance with their prejudices," despite the efforts of Swedish activists (Boëthius 1989). Within the highly centralized state, the ability of Swedish women to demand reform of the criminal justice system was compromised. In addition, their success in educating the public concerning rape was

---

31. In American states that repealed marital-rape exemptions, the numbers are similarly low. For example, in New Jersey there were only five prosecutions of marital rape within three years after the legislation went into effect. All of these cases involved separated spouses. New Jersey has a population of nine million, one million more than Sweden (Bienen 1983, 144).

marginal compared to that of their American contemporaries, who clearly benefited from having established a mass movement.

For those in Sweden who do not choose to pursue their case through the criminal justice system and would prefer, instead, to receive the support of *autonomous* rape crisis centers, there are none. The established social service and medical communities may try to provide an alternative, yet even the state has recognized that these sectors lack sufficient competence concerning sexual abuse.

An ambivalence toward the provision of rape-related services persists. This was well expressed by a Swedish prosecutor who explained, "we don't think it is natural that rape happens, so we don't tell [women] what to do when it happens" (Qwist, interview, 1988). It was not uncommon for Swedish women to remark caustically that "in Sweden, women can't be raped because we are equal." Swedes are unwilling to address this problem openly. The relative absence of a strong feminist movement, attributable to the centralized state and a deferential society, assures they will not be forced to do so.

In Sweden, rape generally is regarded as both a foreign problem and an issue falling within the jurisdiction of state employees. State-appointed bureaucrats and researchers readily claimed expertise concerning rape. With such knowledge, they were in an excellent position to defend the state against its critics, attribute rape to an "ethnic under-class," and restrain more progressive appeals. Women's sections within the political parties discouraged attempts at self-organization and direct action. There were no separate conferences or speak-outs to provide raped women, as women, a platform from which they could express their grievances and press for reforms that may have better met their needs. Rape-related initiatives were channeled through political parties. Proposed reforms grandiosely called for increased responsiveness, but action rarely followed the rhetoric. For example, Swedish rape reforms never expressly prohibited the introduction of a woman's sexual history in court, and the establishment of legal aides has not increased conviction rates.

By contrast, traditional American rape law was more misogynistic, but those most harmed could effectively mobilize to reform it. This was facilitated by an ardent and independent feminist movement. Legislative reform was brought to the state by women from within this movement. In addition, this same movement mobilized to create a wide range of direct services for raped women. While American state intervention resulted in the professionalization of this movement, the fragmented structure of the state and its pervasive culture of pluralism nonetheless permitted some segments of the anti-rape movement to retain their autonomy. Consequently, women in the United States have benefited from a wider range of legal and support services than have been made available to Swedish women.

 5

STATE INTERVENTION AND SEXUAL HARASSMENT

The comparative analysis of the state's policies, programs, and public statements concerning woman battering and rape presented thus far supports a theory in which the centralization of state power, which apparently promotes Sweden's innovative response to work-related issues, hinders its pursuit of reforms analyzed in gendered terms.[1] This analysis also reveals that the fragmented American state, which is notoriously hostile to labor issues, can be more responsive than Sweden to claims specifically beneficial to women.

Yet, an important question remains: can the Swedish state better respond to a gender-specific issue when it is clearly work-related? If so, then the structure of the American state would function best only for those issues that have no direct consequence for women as workers. To answer this question, one needs to examine each state's response to the work-related and gender-specific issue of sexual harassment.[2]

Like woman battering and rape, sexual harassment constitutes a gender-specific violation of women's bodily integrity. The abuse is perpetrated by men.[3] And, "although some women may be more vulnerable to sexual harassment than others, no woman is immune"

---

1. It can be argued that workers, in general, benefitted from centralization because the corporatist state has been dominated by organized labor, particularly under Social Democratic rule. Yet, as we will discover, the responsiveness of organized labor to work-related issues does not necessarily translate to greater support for gender-specific issues.

2. Sexual harassment is commonly understood as "the imposition of unwelcome sexual demands or the creation of sexually offensive environments" (Rhode 1989, 231). Although sexual harassment occurs in a variety of contexts, it is most often associated with the workplace. Although the focus here will be on harassment at work, it is important to note that women are also sexually harassed at school, in hospitals, on the streets, within their homes and elsewhere.

3. The National Association of Working Women reports that an estimated 90 percent of harassment cases involve men who have harassed women, 9 percent involve same-sex harassment (e.g., heterosexual men harassing gay men), and only 1 percent involve women who have harassed men (Bravo and Cassedy 1992, 64).

(Evans 1978, 207). Indeed, within both states sexual harassment is common.[4] Women are sexually harassed because they are women and not because they are workers. After all, women are also subjected to this abuse outside of the labor market. Moreover, the fact that men often sexually harass their female co-workers suggests that the abuse cannot merely be attributed to another hierarchy (e.g., work). Sexual harassment helps perpetuate gender inequality, particularly at work.

Unlike rape and battery, sexual harassment in the workplace provides an important means of bridging a discussion of women's (sexual) subordination with more conventional texts that focus primarily on women as wage earners. Sexual harassment at work diminishes "woman's potential for social equality in two interpenetrated ways: by using her employment position to coerce her sexually, while using her sexual position to coerce her economically" (MacKinnon 1979, 7).

While feminists and state bureaucrats in Sweden and the United States acknowledge that sexual harassment plays a significant role in occupational segregation, it is remarkable that comparative scholars on women and the labor market have failed to make this connection central to or even explicit in their work. Instead, they attribute the ghettoization of women in part-time, menial, and low-paying jobs either to a lack of job skills or to childcare and other household obligations (e.g., Adams and Winston 1980; Gelb 1990; Jenson, Hagen, and Reddy 1988; Ruggie 1984 and 1987).

Consequently, these scholars suggest that the most effective means of desegregating the labor market is through innovative, state-sponsored, quality childcare and alternative job-training programs. These solutions, however, have proven inadequate (Elman 1993a; Farley 1978; Leghorn and Parker 1981).

If women are to obtain sexual equality, the assertion that childcare is a "woman's issue" needs to be challenged at a fundamental level.[5] Alone, childcare programs cannot remedy occupational segregation. Indeed, they may further perpetuate the sexual division of

---

4. In the United States, a government study found that 42 percent of women were sexually harassed at work over a two year period (U.S. Merit Systems Protection Board 1980). In a less comprehensive study, Swedish authorities revealed that nearly 20 percent of women were sexually harassed at work (JÄMO 1987a). These data will be discussed further.

5. Relabeling "maternity leave" as "parental leave" and making it available to men accomplishes little because so few men have chosen to take primary responsibility for childcare. In Sweden, in 1984, 94.3 percent of all those taking leave were women (Landau 1987, 77).

labor that they were meant to eliminate—those employed to take care of children are primarily women.[6]

As for alternative job training, while this training provides women with the necessary skills to enter male professions, many women leave once they have worked within these fields. Their decisions to withdraw are related to more than socialization, inadequate training, or limited childcare. Sexual harassment, which is especially common in male-dominated work areas, creates intolerable working conditions for women (Farley 1978; Hagman 1988; JÄMO 1987a; MacKinnon 1979).[7] Economist Martha J. Langelan explains: men employ sexual harassment to "define whole sections of our geography and social structure, from public corners to high-wage 'male' technical jobs, as a gender-controlled territory where women can only venture at their own risk" (1993, 40). Such abuse functions to keep women out of male-dominated job areas and reinforces the desirability of menial, part-time labor. The occurrence of sexual harassment, therefore, diminishes women's presence in the labor market.

Although the consequences of sexual harassment are serious and often devastating, women rarely seek formal redress. There are essentially three reasons for this. First, women are aware that, as women, they are expected to revel in sexual attention.[8] Second, charges of sexual harassment, like those relating to rape, are difficult to prove. Often the occurrence involves the word of one worker against another. Third, while men both perpetrate sexual harassment and are frequently in a position of authority to end it, they are the least likely to consider any behavior to be sexual harassment (Evans 1978; Wadstein, interview, 1988). Women who expose their colleagues and/or superiors may be ostracized for their complaints

---

6. Cross-nationally, childcare is consistently one of the most common jobs for women, along with secretary, shop assistant, and nurse. Whether provided at home or in the wage-labor market, childcare is deemed "women's work."

7. To avoid the men who harass them, women may take sick leaves, seek transfers, or quit their jobs. Quitting is one of the most common strategies "since it permits escape without a scene and, no less important, promises the best chance of obtaining future work" (Farley 1978, 23). They may, however, be economically penalized as a result. In leaving one job for another, women loose the accumulation of benefits associated with seniority and promotion.

Scholars often note that women's "work patterns" or careers may be "interrupted" by family responsibilities, like the decision to have children (Adams and Winston 1980; Gelb 1990; Ruggie 1984). Few explicitly recognize that women's "work patterns" are affected by sexual harassment.

8. Studies show, however, that few women find this type of attention flattering when it occurs in the workplace (Farley 1978, 22–23).

and subjected to continued harassment. For these reasons, many women opt for isolation because they have little faith that the problem can be resolved (Chapman and Chapman 1984a).

Sexual harassment existed long before it was named; women previously regarded it as an unpleasant fact of life, rather than a social condition.[9] Only with women's increased participation in the labor market and the emergence of a feminist consciousness did women note that sexual harassment was a systematic practice. They then named the act, documented its occurrence, and publicly resisted it (Farley 1978; MacKinnon 1979).

Of the three gender-specific case studies presented in this book, sexual harassment is the most recently recognized abuse. American law discreetly overlooked sexual harassment until the 1970s; Swedish law failed to recognize its existence until 1992. This chapter accounts for the difference.

The United States

The Discovery and Documentation of Sexual Harassment

Only two decades ago, one could not find the term "sexual harassment" in the index of even the most radical feminist texts. The earliest references were made in connection with rape in the mid 1970s. Women regarded sexual harassment as the "little rapes" (Tong 1984, 65), in other words, as an everyday violation with which they were forced to contend.[10]

American women first discovered sexual harassment in their discussions with each other. Lin Farley, who was among the first to expose the issue (1978), explains her experience in a 1974 consciousness-raising group devoted to the workplace:

[T]he group was a nearly equal division of black and white, with economic backgrounds ranging from very affluent to poor. Still, when we

---

9. For a brief history of sexual harassment, from slavery through industrialism and to the present, see Farley (1978). Moreover, Langelan reveals that one of the earliest recorded instances of sexual harassment is in the Bible (1993, 64). See the story of Susanna and the Elders in the Book of Daniel.

10. Indeed, it was the Community Action Strategies to Stop Rape (CASSR) project in Columbus, Ohio, that originally developed confrontational strategies to end street sexual harassment. The project did this as part of its rape prevention program, which was funded by a grant from the National Institute for Mental Health. For a history of such activism, a brilliant analysis of sexual harassment, and innovative stories with suggestions on how to effectively confront sexual harassment, read Langelan's *Back Off!* (1993).

had finished, there was an unmistakable pattern to our employment. Something absent from all the literature ... was newly exposed. Each one of us had already quit or been fired from a job at least once because we had been made too uncomfortable by the behavior of men. (1978, xi)

Farley (and others) decided that this behavior required a name and "sexual harassment seemed about as close to symbolizing the problem as the language would permit" (Farley 1978, xi).

Members of the consciousness-raising group soon addressed the issue of sexual harassment in public. They received support from others within the feminist movement. At the time, Eleanor Holmes Norton was Director of the New York City Human Rights Commission and Karen DeCrow was the national president of the National Organization for Women (NOW). These and other women helped establish Working Women United (WWU), which served as a resource center and activist organization "devoted to the needs and problems of women who work outside the home" (Evans 1978, 222, n. 2). WWU's first and primary concern, however, was sexual harassment in the workplace.

On May 4, 1975, WWU held the first Speak Out Against Sexual Harassment in Ithaca, New York. It was an effective means of redefining male behavior as women experienced it. A journalist for *The New York Times* covered the event and later published the first nationally syndicated article concerning sexual harassment (Nemy 1975). Her coverage was essential in promoting an awareness of the problem. Women from all over the United States, including many who had never before identified themselves as feminists, contacted Farley and the others (Farley 1978, xii-xiii).

An anti-sexual harassment network began and was readily incorporated within the existing women's movement. Throughout the country women continued to organize and speak out. At San Diego State University, for example, feminist students organized an "A for a Lay Day" workshop (Farley 1978, 70). NOW chapters organized similar events and provided information on sexual harassment. Within only a few years, a proliferation of surveys emerged both within the women's movement (Craib 1977; Working Women United Institute 1975) and outside of it (*Redbook* 1976). Some surveys found that 20 percent of women had been sexually harassed (Craib 1977), while others projected rates as high as 92 percent (*Redbook* 1976). The differences between these figures can, of course, be attributed to how the studies were conducted and how each defined harassment. Significantly, however, the continued exposure of the problem was essential in providing women with the awareness that they might already have been the victims of it.

The issue of sexual harassment was receiving such attention that, by 1980, the Merit Systems Protection Board (MSPB) conducted the most comprehensive study ever undertaken in the United States concerning sexual harassment at work. Government researchers defined sexual harassment as "deliberate or repeated unsolicited verbal comments, gestures or physical contact of a sexual nature that is considered to be unwelcome by the recipient" (U.S. Merit Systems Protection Board 1981, 2). The board surveyed 23,964 randomly selected federal employees and obtained a response rate of 84 percent (N=20,083). They found that 42 percent of the women surveyed reported being sexually harassed at work in a two year period (U.S. Merit Systems Protection Board 1981, 3). The American government concluded that sexual harassment was pervasive.

On the strength of feminist consciousness, an organized women's movement, and mounting research data, women were in a strong position to pressure the state to recognize sexual harassment as a serious problem and provide remedy. Like civil rights law, sexual harassment law followed only after those who had been harmed documented their injuries and insisted on legal remedy through social and political action.[11]

Legal Battles and Administrative Redress

Feminist lawyers proved vital in the fight against sexual harassment. They launched a series of legal appeals that eventually provided women with formal redress. The first legal actions contested the denial of unemployment compensation for those who had been sexually harassed. Women sought protection from the abysmal financial consequences that resulted from having to leave their jobs. While those who voluntarily leave their jobs are eligible for unemployment benefits if they can prove that they have good cause for quitting,[12]

---

11. Many of the original claimants were African American women. Langelan suggests this is because harassers have long been privileged men, in positions of authority, able to use their power against those women most socially and economically vulnerable. Moreover, white men have historically assaulted African American women with impunity (1993, 66–67). This fact does not, however, imply that African American and Latino men are not also harassers.

12. Employees are not expected to endure situations and/or conditions that endanger their physical or mental health.

state unemployment agencies were reluctant to consider sexual harassment as a reasonable cause of constructive discharge.[13]

To mitigate the bias of state agencies, the WWU helped develop legislation which explicitly states that sexual harassment is a reasonable cause for quitting one's job and that women who quit in the face of harassment should not be denied unemployment compensation. The legislation was first introduced before the New York legislature in 1978; it died in committee. This defeat should not be attributed to organized opposition to the law's passage. Rather, its proponents had failed to define the abuse carefully or clarify why the legislature should enact a special law to provide its victims consideration for unemployment benefits (MacKinnon 1979). A similar bill, providing a more concrete definition of sexual harassment, passed the same year in Wisconsin and was considered by other state legislatures. In addition, activists throughout the country got local human rights commissions and commissions on the status of women to intervene on behalf of sexually harassed women whose unemployment claims had been denied (Farley 1978).

Although significant bias against women remains, most state and local human rights commissions and commissions on the status of women took action against agencies that had refused unemployment benefits to sexually harassed women. They established sexual harassment as "a violation of a woman's right to equal working conditions" and, thus, an appropriate cause for abandoning one's work. By 1978, Farley wrote, "there is no area in the country today that does not have some such complaint in progress" (1978, 127). Within only four years after the problem first received public attention, women could appeal successfully for their benefits. Government officials responded by publicly denouncing sexual harassment at work.

Although the pursuit of fair unemployment compensation proved moderately successful, many standard legal approaches to sexual harassment proved inadequate. Criminal law requires that abuse result in serious physical injury. Feminists noted, that in instances of sexual harassment involving physical assault, the prosecutor would more likely pursue the assailant with rape or assault charges (Tong 1984, 71). In the absence of rape or other physical violence, criminal law does not provide remedy to harassed women.

---

13. Constructive discharge occurs "if the employer deliberately makes an employee's working conditions so intolerable that the employee is forced into involuntary resignation ..." (Vinciguerra 1989, n. 15). For further discussion concerning the general doctrine of constructive discharge in cases of sexual harassment, see Vinciguerra (1989).

Until sexual harassment was specifically recognized as a form of sex discrimination, a woman's only legal option was tort law. Tort law "views sexual harassment as an outrage to an individual woman's sensibilities and society's purported values ..." (Tong 1984, 77). Tort law essentially individualizes, devalues, and pathologizes cases of sexual harassment. By contrast, feminists note that sexual harassment is pervasive and serious and that it is not merely coincidental that it happens to women (Farley 1978; MacKinnon 1979).

In 1975, feminist attorney Catharine A. MacKinnon circulated a manuscript which formulated the legal argument that sexual harassment is sex discrimination (MacKinnon 1979, xi). Defining this abuse as a civil rights violation empowers women to seek legal redress under Title VII of the Civil Rights Act of 1964. The act expressly prohibits discrimination on the basis of race or sex in "terms, conditions, and privileges of employment." Despite the simple brilliance of MacKinnon's argument and, more importantly, the avenue of redress it offered, most courts refused to accept her reasoning at that time.

It was not until 1977 that an American court considered sexual harassment as sex discrimination. The United States Court of Appeals in Washington, D.C., was the first. It reversed a lower court's decision and explicitly acknowledged that a woman "became the target of her superior's sexual desires because she was a woman, and was asked to bow to his demands as the price for holding her job" (*Barnes v. Costle*, 1977). The appeals court found that the sexually harassed woman was entitled to the protection afforded by Title VII of the Civil Rights Act of 1964. As a result, the plaintiff, Barnes, received $18,000 in back pay from the Environmental Protection Agency. This case provided a foundation upon which other victories were established.

By 1980, case precedent favored a legal approach in which sexual harassment was classified as unlawful sex discrimination. The nation's Equal Employment Opportunity Commission (EEOC) instituted guidelines outlining what constitutes illegal sexual harassment under Title VII. The guidelines state:

> Unwelcome sexual advances, requests for sexual favors, and other verbal or physical conduct of a sexual nature constitute sexual harassment when (1) submissions to such conduct are a condition of an individual's employment, (2) submission to or rejection of such conduct by an individual is used as the basis for employment decisions affecting such individual, or (3) such conduct has the purpose or effect of unreasonably interfering with an individual's work

performance or creating an intimidating, hostile, or offensive working environment. (Chapman and Chapman 1984a, 3)

In addition, the EEOC stated that employers would be held responsible for the actions of their harassing employees. Moreover, they were responsible "regardless of whether the specific acts complained of were authorized or even forbidden by the employer and regardless of whether the employer knew or should have known of their occurrence" (Chapman and Chapman 1984a, 3).

In 1986, the Supreme Court reviewed its first case regarding sexual harassment (*Meritor Savings Bank v. Vinson*, 1986). While the court recognized the plaintiff's claim that sexual harassment established a "hostile work environment," it refused to delineate the scope of employer liability (Vinciguerra 1989, 1730). The lower courts were, thus, entrusted to establish these parameters. Contrary to the fears of those who expected otherwise, a thorough investigation of appellate decisions reveals that the courts are providing "solid case law in redressing the rights of sexual harassment victims" (Bennett-Alexander 1991, 85).

By 1993, the Supreme Court was to rule a second time on sexual harassment; it did so unanimously. Again considering the matter of "hostile work environment," the court held that an employee does not have to demonstrate serious injury to prove a "hostile work environment." Rather, the conduct must be "sufficiently severe or pervasive to alter the conditions of the victim's employment and create an abusive environment" (*Harris v. Forklift Systems Inc.* 1993). As with *Meritor*, lower courts are given great latitude through interpretation. However, as they confront the facts of particular cases to determine the meaning of "severe" and "pervasive" misconduct, they will likely rely on compelling precedent for guidance.

The courts have not acted alone. Congress also intervened, and, with the passage of the 1991 Civil Rights Act, compensatory and punitive damages were made available to sexual harassment plaintiffs, up to a maximum of between $55,000 and $300,000, depending on the size of the employer (*Civil Rights Act* 1991). Although these initial acts and regulations were confined to the realm of employment, legislation was soon enacted to extend the right of protection against sexual harassment into other areas, including education.

Parallel to the Title VII ruling for workers, sexual harassment in education became actionable under Title IX; this 1972 amendment to the Civil Rights Act of 1964 bars sex bias in educational institutions receiving federal funds. It could be argued that such congressional action established a firm foundation upon which the Supreme Court would later act. In 1992, the Supreme Court unanimously ruled that, under Title IX, students are permitted to sue for damages resulting from sexual harassment and other forms of discrimination (*Franklin v. Gwinnett County Public Schools*, 1992). As with all legal reforms, those pertaining to sexual harassment have both reflected and shaped acceptable standards of behavior (Chamallas 1992). Once the law determined that sexual harassment was illegal, women were formally permitted to resist and complain about it. As Deborah Rhode states, "Judicial recognition has been critical in legitimating the injuries that stem from harassment and transforming a personal problem into a political issue" (1989, 236).

Additionally, legal reform encouraged the establishment of quasi-legal policies against sexual harassment. In an attempt to reduce their liability and enhance their public reputations, firms and institutions throughout the country have begun writing anti-harassment policies. They are creating internal training programs and grievance procedures for preventing harassment and handling complaints as they arise (Gambon 1989).[14] The recent United States Senate Judiciary confirmation hearings in which law professor Anita Hill confronted Supreme Court nominee Clarence Thomas with the charge of sexual harassment served to further such efforts by dramatically bringing the issue to the forefront.[15] Following the hearings, statutes are pending in several states that would require employers to provide a harassment policy and educational programs to workers (Salholz 1992, 22).

While it has unquestionably benefited women to have access to legal redress, making sexual harassment illegal has not entirely remedied the problem. A growing number of women are reporting the abuse. Yet, some note that the test of "an effective approach to sexual harassment and sex discrimination" is "whether there is a

---

14. According to a recent survey of Fortune 500 companies, each year sexual harassment costs a typical large business $6.7 million in litigation and settlements (Gambon 1989).

15. The editors of *Ms.* expanded the letters column in the January/February 1992 issue to provide room for the readers' letters expressing support for Anita Hill and outrage that so many members of the general public had not believed her (1992, 8–11). For an excellent collection of essays concerning the sexual and racial politics of Hill's testimony before the Senate Judiciary Committee, see Morrison (1992).

Additionally, as public awareness increased, many business firms reviewed their existing policies against harassment and implemented new ones. A 1992 survey of Fortune 500 companies found that 81 percent offer sensitivity programs, up from 60 percent in 1988 (Salholz 1992, 22).

surge of complaints" (Chapman and Chapman 1984b, 10). After all, the state's apparent responsiveness may increase the number of women willing to report harassment. If the state can effectively deal with this increase, a reduction of complaints may follow as the actual incidence of sexual harassment declines (Chapman and Chapman 1984b).

In the end, the state may prove incapable of providing women with the redress activists had expected. Indeed, women have often been disappointed. The EEOC, which has been the major government agency responsible for mitigating sex and race discrimination, has recognized far more subtle instances of race discrimination than sex discrimination (Chapman and Chapman 1984a; MacKinnon 1979). In addition, the agency has been so deluged with complaints that it is incapable of efficiently pursuing all of them (Lavelle 1989).

Advocates for sexually harassed women have not, however, relied solely on any one of the state's particular avenues of redress, such as courts or commissions. Few women have the money, time, and legal counsel necessary to win in court. More importantly, research indicates that women prefer to resolve the problem without having to resort to formal channels outside of the workplace (U.S. Merit Systems Protection Board 1981). For this reason, feminists helped establish alternative grievance procedures and educational programs for businesses and educational institutions. Lastly, in a manner consistent with their political culture (discussed in Chapter 2), an increasing number of women in the United States are pursuing confrontational strategies that directly hold individual perpetrators responsible (Langelan 1993). Such actions include nonviolent personal and group confrontation techniques.

Women's ability to obtain alternative remedies rests, in part, on the capacity of the American state to insist on such options. Through its courts, agencies, commissions, and acts, the state has held some employers and institutions liable. This can often be financially burdensome. Thus, companies and institutions have been encouraged to provide internal avenues of redress while taking necessary steps to discourage sexual harassment from occurring. "In recognizing sexual harassment as a legal claim," the American state legitimized women's resistance to sexual violation and "provided a mechanism of accountability for their violators" (MacKinnon in Langelan 1993, 14).

Sexual harassment became a politicized issue fairly recently, dating only from the 1970s. Much remains to be done and more analysis is needed before women can better determine which approaches are most effective. Still, because there is a strong feminist movement to sustain such efforts and the state has, over time, responded to its requests, there is reason to believe that efforts on behalf of sexually harassed women will continue in the United States.

Sweden

The Identification of Sexual Harassment

Swedish women identified sexual harassment a decade after American women had documented and protested its existence. This does not, of course, mean that the abuse did not exist previously. As in the United States, the behavior had yet to acquire a name.[16]

Unlike American women, most Swedish women did not learn about sexual harassment from each other. It was brought to the public's attention by state officials who were charged with equality issues. As Maud Eduards explains, "The prevailing norm in Sweden for furthering sex/gender equality maintains that women and men should work together, on a non-conflictual basis, within the traditional party system" (1992, 102). Consequently, Swedish feminists often work for reforms within governmental bureaucracies and/or the women's sections of the parties rather than in autonomous women's projects and organizations.

In the absence of consciousness-raising and an autonomous feminist movement, it is not surprising that the public discourse concerning sexual harassment came from within the centralized state and not from outside of it. Yet, it would be politically naive to view this initiative as an indicator of the state's responsiveness to sexually harassed women.

In 1979, the Riksdag passed the Swedish Act on Equality Between Women and Men at Work (Equal Opportunities Act). Like Title VII of the 1964 Civil Rights Act, it is restricted to the workplace and forbids employers to discriminate against an employee or job applicant on the basis of gender. In contrast to American law, the act does not recognize the possibility of sex discrimination among co-workers.[17] Additionally, Sweden has no anti-sex discrimination

16. In 1988, I met with Cecilia Önfelt, an active member of the Center Party and a self-proclaimed feminist. She recounted having met Letty Pogrebin, an editor for *Ms*. It was 1982, and Pogrebin asked about sexual harassment. Önfelt explained that, at the time, no one understood her question. "Now we know what she meant," Önfelt explained (interview, 1988).

17. This is not surprising, given the strength of predominantly male unions and their historical reticence in acknowledging gender conflict as politically significant.

policies that extend beyond the labor market. Consequently, women are without legal protection in areas such as education, in which American law provides women redress through Title IX.

The 1980 Equal Opportunities Act established an ombudsman (Jämställdhetsombudsman) [sic] to ensure its enforcement. The Equality Ombudsman's Office (JÄMO) soon determined that many people bringing complaints were sexually harassed women. Indeed, JÄMO tried harassment cases under the existing Equal Opportunities Act, but without success. The deputy ombudsman attributed this failure to the consciousness of the courts: "I feel like in each case I had to prove the earth is round" (Wadstein, interview, 1988). JÄMO concluded that the Act provides inadequate redress to sexually harassed women.

Before addressing the particular shortcomings of the Equal Opportunities Act in affording remedy to sexually harassed women, it is important to examine the additional reasons for its general ineffectiveness. Anti-discrimination policies were opposed by the Social Democrats and the unions for nearly a decade. The act's passage was assured only by a three-party, nonsocialist coalition that briefly interrupted Social Democratic rule from 1976–1982. Although all parties, including the Social Democrats, now support the Act,[18] the original opposition of organized labor and the left coalition had important consequences.

Fearful of losing its primacy within the corporatist bargaining structure, labor allowed the Act's passage only after the political parties permitted the unions' collective agreements with employers to take precedence over the legal provisions of the Act. Consequently, the ombudsman's role in advocacy and supervision of the Act was limited to the 10 percent of the labor market where collective agreements do not exist. In other words, it was assumed that labor unions will provide the primary venue for legal recourse.

The limited nature of JÄMO's power has been openly acknowledged, even by the ombudsman (SOU 1990:41). The former deputy ombudsman, Margareta Wadstein, said, "We can only ask a court to fine employers ... if they have no equality agreements ... most complaints we receive come from women who work in places bound by collective agreements. So we have to refer them back to their union for help" (interview, 1988). Consequently, JÄMO has

---

18. This may explain the tendency of numerous scholars to applaud and credit the Social Democrats or left with Sweden's equality policy (e.g., Norris 1987; Verba 1987) despite the fact that it did not originate under their rule.

been directly responsible for very few sex discrimination cases.[19] Moreover, the "unions insist that women's problems stem from their being workers and not from being women" (Wadstein, interview, 1988). This attitude is exacerbated by another important factor: unions are often unwilling to pursue sex discrimination cases that involve other (male) union employees. This reluctance to acknowledge sexual harassment claims involving union members promotes false solidarity at great expense to women workers.

Organized labor, together with the parties, effectively denied JÄMO the interventionist powers necessary to pursue sex equality rigorously. The act was based on the voluntary compliance of 90 percent of the labor market. This sector was expected to promote sexual equality, with no recourse offered when the expectation is disappointed. Consequently, "equality was recommended, not mandated" (Eduards 1988, 12). Or perhaps better said, gender inequality was not effectively interdicted.

Shortly before completing its tenure, the conservative government expanded the ombudsman's powers by revising the Equal Opportunities Act. As of July 1994, the ombudsman will oversee all areas of the wage labor market. It is too soon to render a judgement as to what the effects of this change will be.

The resistance of both Social Democrats and organized labor to legislation intended specifically to benefit women workers compromises the conventional assertion that women can depend on labor to pursue their interests. Similarly, it is misguided to portray the Social Democrats as a trusted promoter of women's liberation (Elman 1993a). Moreover, despite the 1994 revision, the continued reluctance of the political establishment (both left and right) to adopt specific policies against sexual harassment reveals that women *qua* women are without a dependable ally within Sweden's corporatist state.

Having noted the general difficulties for women pursuing claims of sex discrimination, one can better appreciate the additional problems faced by those who have been sexually harassed. Like American women, women in Sweden are permitted legal redress for harassment through criminal law but only if it occurs in a public

19. From 1980 to 1990, the ombudsman brought only thirty-six cases before the Labor Court and lost approximately two-thirds of them. The Equal Opportunities Commission established by the Act to render decisions concerning possible infringements made by employers not subject to collective agreements did not rule on a single case in ten years. Five cases had been withdrawn, however, and nearly fifty other disputes were resolved through arbitration (SOU 1990:41).

place and results in a socially and legally recognizable harm like physical assault and/or rape. Alone, sexual harassment is not recognized as harmful enough to warrant criminal redress. Thus, Swedish prosecutors, like American prosecutors, are unlikely to pursue sexual harassment claims through criminal channels. And, in sharp contrast to the Americans, Swedes rarely bring civil suits (Kelman 1981).[20] Cases involving labor disputes go to special labor courts, not civil courts. Consequently, the Swedish legal system is distinguished from its American counterpart in that it creates a context in which employers are not likely to be threatened with severe penalties for their failure to confront sexual harassment.

Even the revised Equal Opportunities Act of 1994 does not afford protection to women harassed by co-workers. As noted earlier, the Act covers only employer/employee relations in which the centralized corporatist state acknowledges conflict to exist. Additionally, unless sex discrimination results in a disadvantageous distribution of duties or dismissal, no harm is considered to have occurred. Sexual harassment is *per se* legally unrecognizable as a distinct form of abuse.

In 1987, JÄMO launched the first Swedish survey on the scope and distinctiveness of sexual harassment as a harm at work. JÄMO surveyed 4,220 women whose addresses were derived from member lists of nine unions representing both workers and salaried employees in the public and private sector. Nearly half of the women who received the survey responded (N=2,108). To date, it remains the only original Swedish survey research on the subject.[21] This study (The "FRID-A" Projekt) found that nearly 20 percent of the respondents had been sexually harassed at work. This was much lower than the 42 percent of American women sampled by the U.S. government who stated that they had been harassed within the last two years. These figures may actually reflect the true rate of incidence; yet, there are several reasons to doubt this. First, the American study was more extensive and had a higher response rate.[22] Second, one must appreciate the effect that the American women's movement had on the ability of women in the United

---

20. As was noted in Chapter 2, litigiousness is structurally rebuffed in Sweden. One need only consider the reliance on ombudsmen who require that conflicting parties reach compromise. Unlike Americans, Swedes are renowned for avoiding conflict (Daun 1989).

21. New research is examining sexual harassment within higher education, however (Borgblad 1992).

22. The American response rate was 84 percent of 23,964 (N=20,083).

States to note that they had been sexually harassed. In Sweden, there was no similar movement to promote an awareness of the abuse. The public discourse concerning sexual harassment began only *after* JÄMO issued its findings. There were no speak-outs, consciousness-raising groups, or other forums from which to publicly address and protest this inequality. Last, and perhaps more important, in the absence of any legal redress, silence may have surfaced as the preferred coping strategy.

After releasing its study, the Office of the Equality Ombudsman insisted that sexual harassment in Sweden was a significant problem. The ombudsman claimed that the survey's findings were similar to several American studies. Of those harassed, few requested any help from their union or personnel department, despite the fact that many claimed that they had suffered physically and/or mentally. As in the United States, women disclosed that they kept silent for fear of reprisal. Those who did complain said that they had suffered retaliation at work. One-third of all those sexually harassed stated that they had to leave their place of employment.

The FRID-A project explicitly made the connection between sexual harassment and occupational segregation by sex: "Sexual harassment is an assertion of power that men use to keep women out of male-dominated jobs and to keep women in female-dominated working places down" (JÄMO 1987b, 3). Despite numerous state investments in nontraditional occupational-training programs for women, Sweden's wage-labor market remains highly segregated.[23] This challenges the notion that occupational segregation can be overcome merely by providing women with the skills necessary for traditional male jobs.

The ombudsman concluded her report to the government with a summary of actions taken by the United States to end sexual harassment (JÄMO 1987a). At the time, "hardly anything worth telling had been done in Sweden ..." (Hagman 1992b, 3). It was, thus, noted that "The United States is 10 years ahead of Sweden

23. Recent government surveys of fifty-two occupational fields showed that only five had an equal distribution of men and women in 1990. Moreover, in thirteen fields, at least 90 percent of the employees were of the same sex (Swedish Institute 1993, 3). An earlier government report revealed that approximately 80 percent of all wage-earning women are employed in eleven occupations. Women are employed primarily in the service, health care, and office sectors. The most common jobs for women are childcare worker, secretary, shop assistant, office cleaner, and nurse (SOU 1979:56). In assessing the impact of the Equal Opportunities Act, the government found no evidence to suggest that conditions had significantly changed for women (SOU 1990:41).

when it comes to measures against sexual harassment in working life" (JÄMO 1987a, 3).

Legal Remedy Requested and Redress Deferred

JÄMO estimates that hundreds of thousands of the two million women in the labor market experience sexual harassment and claims that this harassment constitutes a threat to "women's economy, health and pleasure in work" (JÄMO 1987a, 6). The ombudsman, therefore, suggested that the Equal Opportunities Act be amended to include a legal definition of sexual harassment. Like American women, Swedish women understood that legislative recognition provides a context within which women can assert violation. Moreover, they believed in the power of the law to transform consciousness so that sexual harassment would no longer be condoned as socially acceptable and/or insignificant. They wished to stigmatize it as unjust.

Although JÄMO requested that the government amend the act to prohibit sexual harassment, it failed to propose any specific suggestions. The government responded to JÄMO's request for an amendment by launching an investigation into the effectiveness of the entire Act. Yet, by incorporating sexual harassment into a general discussion of "worker" equality policy, the issue, from a feminist perspective, was greatly depoliticized.

In 1990, the government released its investigation of the Equal Opportunities Act (SOU 1990:41). It noted that the Act provided little substantive change for working women and that much needed to be done to obtain sexual equality in the Swedish wage-labor market. The report essentially confirmed what Swedish women had long known and what many foreign researchers had chosen to ignore: on issues specifically beneficial to women, the state was anything but innovative. The state's approach to sexual equality is best characterized by cautious restraint.[24]

In its cursory discussion of sexual harassment, the government emphasized existing avenues of remedy for complainants. It stated that "serious" instances of sexual harassment "must be approached under the provisions of the Criminal Code" (SOU 1990:41, 38).

---

24. For instance, while many requested that the anti-discrimination policies be extended to include areas such as education, the government insisted that "educators should be given time to show that ... equality work is being carried out" (SOU 1990:41, 34).

The investigation failed to note, however, that with the exception of rape or assault, "serious" cases of sexual harassment have never been successfully pursued by these means. For less "serious" cases, the government insists that sexual harassment be considered a "work environment" problem and that it be addressed through the Occupational Safety and Health Act, which was essentially established to promote a positive, healthy work atmosphere for employees. This Act neither provides a definition of sexual harassment nor mentions sex discrimination in any way. It is, therefore, difficult to comprehend what meaningful redress the Occupational Safety and Health Act could provide. Although sexual harassment certainly contributes to a pernicious working environment for women, no harassment case has been successfully pursued through this channel either.

The government did concede, however, that there are situations where sexually harassed women have little remedy. "There are forms of sexual harassment where a demand for, or suggestion of, sexual compliance, is tied to threats of disadvantages at work, or to a promise of certain privileges" (SOU 1990:41, 38).

To counteract these particular instances, the government merely amended the Equal Opportunities Act. The Act now reads: "An employer may not subject an employee to harassment because the latter has rejected the employer's sexual advances or lodged a complaint about the employer for sex discrimination" (Ds 1992:92, 14). Ninni Hagman, one of the authors of the FRID-A report, perceptively notes that this amendment does not specifically prohibit sexual harassment. She writes:

> Not until he ... punishes her for rejecting his sexual advances with some *other* kind of harassment, such as failing to raise her wages or unwanted changes in working conditions, is he considered to be subjecting her to sex discrimination. (Hagman 1992b, 12)

Far from winning accolades for this amendment, the government received a series of criticisms (mostly from feminists) that revealed the shortcomings of the reform (Dahlberg 1993; Hagman 1992b). Critics noted, for example, that the law fails to provide relief to women harassed by co-workers. Unless harassment results in a disadvantageous distribution of duties or dismissal, no harm is legally considered to have occurred. Consequently, sexual harassment is legally unrecognizable as a distinct abuse that is intrinsically prejudicial. The specific injuries that stem from such abuse are essentially concealed. Even with the adoption of the 1994 Equal

Opportunities Act, these shortcomings persist. It is, therefore, unlikely that this latest reform will dramatically advance the position of Swedish women.

Summary

In the United States, sexual harassment was discovered by women themselves, who noted that they were the victims of it. American women promoted change through courts, commissions, agencies, and their own organizations, such as the National Organization for Women and Working Women United. Initially, they had limited success in requesting remedies that specifically recognize the distinct harm of sexual harassment. Yet, within less than five years, they had garnered such widespread support that the federal government defined and specifically prohibited the abuse. In addition, employers and educational institutions are pursuing programs to lessen its frequency, and the courts formally recognize sexual harassment as discrimination based on sex.

The Swedish case offers a stunning contrast. State bureaucrats within the Equality Ombudsman's Office were the first to publicly address sexual harassment—a decade after their American counterparts. These officials openly acknowledge the influence American anti-harassment advocates had on their ability to detect and define the problem (Hagman 1988; JÄMO 1987a; Wadstein, interview, 1988). Without an *autonomous* feminist movement (i.e., one that is independent of the state and/or parties and unions), Swedish women had no extensive, independent network to discuss and challenge the conditions of their working lives as women.

After the Equality Ombudsman's Office began to address sexual harassment, the issue was incorporated into a general discussion of working conditions. The Swedish state regards sexual harassment more as a "working environment" issue than an issue of sexual inequality. The failure of Sweden's policy makers to address sexual harassment as an issue of sexual abuse and inequality reflects a crucial weakness in their gender-neutral approach to issues involving gender equity.

The influence of labor within the centralized state proved vital in subsuming sexual harassment under the more general discussions of work. In the words of Ninni Hagman, this relative silence is not surprising: "Sexual harassment is a delicate subject and the closer we come to discussing our own world [Sweden], the more we seem to deny the problem exists" (1992b, 16).[25] This situation has caused the deputy ombudsman to remark that "all that involves a discussion of sexuality [i.e., gender] is taboo" (Wadstein, interview 1988). Put somewhat differently, "sex is not openly acknowledged as a politically relevant basis for competing interests" (Jónasdóttir 1988, 44).

The only Swedish legislation remotely able to offer assistance to sexually harassed women is the Equal Opportunities Act, which prohibits sex discrimination in the workplace. The existence of sexual discrimination within other contexts has been largely ignored so that even Sweden's educational institutions provide no redress. Given a distaste for litigation, the lack of civil courts (or reliance on labor courts), the circumscribed power of the ombudsman to enforce the Act, and the continued reluctance of the powerful unions to address the issue, women are without a powerful, autonomous means or agency that can effectively intervene on their behalf. Consequently, Sweden's existing sex discrimination policies promote only conditional liberation: women are free to work as workers but only within the confines of a segregated labor market in which they are not effectively guaranteed freedom from the sexual harassment that they are subjected to as women.

Sweden's labor market remains one of the most occupationally segregated in Europe (Hagman 1992b). Swedes often remark that, because women and men receive the same salaries for identical jobs, women and men have different jobs (Wistrand 1981, 53). Because occupational segregation is so pervasive, traditional indicators like male/female wage ratios do not accurately reflect women's position within the work force as a whole.[26]

An analysis of sexual harassment in the workplace is central to a better understanding of women's position within the labor market. Without such an analysis, any nation risks pursuing only those approaches to sexual equality that have already proven insufficient, such as job-training programs. Moreover, if we fail to recognize the

---

25. Such denial dramatically diminishes the ability of individuals who otherwise might have disclosed their abuse. Consequently, estimations of actual rates of sexual harassment remain conservative. Surveys of this problem are, thus, insufficient.

26. In 1984, the average full-time female American worker received 63 percent as much as the average male full-time American worker (U.S. Bureau of the Census 1984, table 31, 113). In 1982, the average full-time female Swedish worker earned 80 percent as much as her male counterpart. Yet, if we include all Swedish workers, both part-time and full-time, the average female worker earned 64 percent as much as the average male worker (Statistics Sweden 1986, tables 211 and 212, 211). At the decade's close, gendered differentials increased (Statistics Sweden 1990, 53).

effects of sexual harassment, it appears that conditions like occupational segregation by sex will remain "curiously impervious to change" (Ruggie 1987, 264). Finally, the more conventional assumption that sexual harassment is a private or personal problem obscures the significance of its role in maintaining sexual inequality, particularly at work.

Sweden's lack of legislative recognition and remedy for sexual harassment provides one of the most compelling challenges to the conventional characterization of the Swedish state as interventionist, innovative, and egalitarian. Sweden prides itself on promoting gender equality and excellent working conditions but has failed to mitigate those conditions that are specifically disadvantageous to women.

6

Conclusion

While the American state is widely characterized as resistant to the development of innovative social policies, the Swedish state is portrayed as more humane and one in which "the reforming spirit never sleeps" (Heclo and Madsen 1987, 6).[1] The structure of these states frequently provides a central explanation for their differences. The fragmented and decentralized structure of the American state is regarded as largely responsible for impeding the development and implementation of policies especially beneficial to the disadvantaged. By contrast, the corporatist and centralized structure of the Swedish state is credited with encouraging socioeconomic policies that diminish hardship.

Although generalizations concerning the capacities of any state are vulnerable to empirical exceptions, my objection to them is more theoretical. As noted earlier, it is unwise to assume that the strengths and weaknesses of states remain constant for a variety of social policies. It is similarly misguided to assume that patriarchal states have no variance, that one patriarchal state is like any other. And, given the patriarchal orthodoxy of social science, it is not surprising that the specific oppression that occurs in the daily lives of women has been excluded from the scope of seemingly universal arguments concerning American and Swedish social policy and state structure.

On the basis of case studies relating specifically to woman battering, rape and sexual harassment, I assert quite a different argument concerning the capacities of these states: While Sweden may advance more innovative social policies to counter the most harmful effects of class inequality, its centralized state rebuffs intervention on behalf of women and denies the importance of gendered conflicts. Conversely, the United States may be less able to promote favorable labor policies, but its fragmented federalist state is more

1. Heclo and Madsen do concede, however, that "It has always been foreigners, rather than the Swedes themselves, who have erected abstract notions of a Swedish model for successful democratic government." Yet the "Swedes have typically relished and over time promoted this view of themselves" (1987, 31).

permeable than Sweden to requests for novel solutions to gender-specific oppression. The ability of the American state to innovate effectively has consistently been underestimated, while Sweden's ability to do the same has often been exaggerated. This is largely because the locus of so much political analysis on both states is on the harms that men suffer. Class inequities and racism disadvantage men as well as women, while lowering the threshold of male privilege. By contrast, gender inequality benefits men as a group and disempowers women, including those women who benefit from class and race privilege. Mainstream political analysis has been dramatically distorted by the patriarchal lenses through which it views the Swedish and American states.

Woman battering, rape, and sexual harassment are pervasive and have traumatic social consequences. Women are effectively denied fundamental human rights, such as their right to bodily and emotional integrity. Society begins to accept the denial of these rights as a cultural given and/or politically insignificant. Evidence suggests that these abuses are so widespread that they appear normal. These acts invoke terror and are almost universally committed by men. Stated simply, woman battering, rape, and sexual harassment constitute a systematic context of women's subordination. By taking action against these occurrences, states then serve the interests of women.

Women in Sweden and the United States have sought to mobilize their respective states against their subjection. In both states, women have established programs and policies that provide them greater opportunities for redress and protection from the men who abuse them. They have also worked to prevent abuse from occurring. The growing interest in gender-specific abuse and the actions taken against it permit an analysis of these conditions as socially and politically significant.

Throughout this work, I have insisted that the structure of these states greatly influences the ways in which Swedish and American activists pursue their objectives. In turn, the ways in which they organize affect the kinds of policies and programs that result from their efforts.

Sweden

The political culture of deference and the highly centralized structure of the Swedish state discourage the initiation of policy reforms by nonelites. Therefore, it is not surprising that, instead of pursuing their interests through feminist projects and organizations that are external to the state, Swedish women have relied upon partisan alliances and state bureaucracies to further their interests as women.[2] In turn, the state is able to extend its reach and control of public discourse concerning women's subordination.

Having effectively circumscribed the parameters of what sexual equality is, the Swedish state readily claims responsibility for having nearly achieved such equality.[3] The state, as opposed to a feminist movement or particular women's organization, enjoys an authoritative voice and self-proclaimed expertise concerning the condition of women. For example, the Equality Ombudsman's Office (JÄMO) was the first to publicly address the issue of sexual harassment. Sweden's only rape crisis center operated under the auspices of the government's agency on sex education (RFSU). The next clinic will be established within a university hospital and will serve as a "national resource center." Individuals publicly opposing women's sexual subordination are brusquely dismissed and often ridiculed. Feminism is either denigrated as "sex racism" (Eduards 1992, 87) or as a front for other political agendas. For example, one male journalist recently declared that the "new feminism" of the 1990s is "just another word for socialism" (Nycander 1993).

Although the National Organization of Emergency Shelters for Battered Women in Sweden (ROKS) is not officially affiliated with a particular party or state bureaucracy, its autonomy is tenuous.[4] Like most other national organizations, ROKS depends entirely on state funding and the continued political support of political parties. One can, therefore, appreciate its caution in challenging the government's authoritative discussion of women's oppression. Continued restraint, however, arrests both innovation and the courage to promote the

2. Although feminist concerns are of central importance in this study, the same situation exists for other unconventional interests, for example, environmentalists and gay male activists.
    Lesbians remain a politically invisible force in both states. One could, however, argue that American lesbians do have a somewhat greater social and political presence than their Swedish counterparts. For more analysis on lesbians in both states, see Rebecka Lindau's article in *off our backs* (1993).
3. By contrast, the American state suffers from a less stellar reputation, perhaps because it has proven less adept at coopting feminist aspirations and initiatives.
4. It is worthy of note that, in 1991, the Social Democratic leaders extended an invitation to Ebon Kram, the chair of ROKS, to join the party. Given its earlier opposition to the Equal Opportunities Act and various other policies, the party suffers from a tarnished reputation concerning programs specifically beneficial to women (Elman 1993a). The Social Democrats wished to correct this, particularly after their fall from power in 1991.

improvements necessary for a more dynamic and responsive political system. Consequently, change-oriented organizations, like ROKS, and their constituencies are seriously disadvantaged.

Forging alliances with the political establishment compromised the energies and effectiveness of those especially devoted to ending women's sexual oppression. Sweden's left parties and well-organized labor movement, though repeatedly depicted as the vanguard of women's rights, often proved unreliable allies (Elman 1993a). For example, both the Social Democratic Party and the unions originally opposed the adoption of the Equal Opportunities Act. Class issues generally dominated the political agenda, while those pertaining to women's physical and sexual abuse were often neglected. Sweden's gender-specific reforms were usually adopted years after the United States had implemented similar acts. The state still refuses to recognize sexual harassment as a distinct abuse worth mobilizing against. Furthermore, Sweden's battering and rape programs and reforms are best characterized as weak and reserved.

Consistently, reforms were drafted by ministerial bureaucrats who had little direct knowledge of the very abuses they were attempting to mitigate.[5] A central component of feminist method, theory, and practice is the notion that women are the experts on their own subordination. Failure to appreciate this often leads to grave error. For example, Sweden's two laws pertaining to battering afford women only a modicum of relief, because their enforcement remains discretionary. Action has never been mandated, although it should have been, considering the prior reluctance of the criminal justice system to intervene on behalf of battered women.

Even Sweden's earliest (1965) and most progressive reform, which outlawed rape in marriage, was ineffectual. In the absence of a rape crisis movement, the public's conception of rape, like its conception of other women's problems, continues unaltered, and authorities are reluctant to intervene. To date, rape is largely regarded as a problem for which immigrants, not Swedes, are responsible. Moreover, policy development remains almost exclusively in the hands of bureaucracies, without significant input from feminists, thereby assuring that the policy goals established are consistently conservative.

Swedish women lack a more powerful and autonomous avenue through which they can both pursue their own (gender-specific) agendas and bring charges against the state for its negligence in

5. Similarly, studies pertaining to women abuse were conducted within state agencies or state-appointed commissions. The researchers were typically bureaucrats who likewise lack a significant understanding of the issues they were investigating.

effectively pursuing those reforms it chooses to adopt. For example, to sue the state for negligence remains structurally impossible. Swedish women are dependent on political parties and ministries to place their issues on the political agenda. Similarly, they rely on state-appointed ombudsmen [sic] to secure a greater commitment from authorities to pursue actions favorable to them. Yet, even the most sympathetic ombudsman has proven too weak to exact meaningful penalties that could ensure the compliance of remiss authorities. Whether the new Equal Opportunities Act (1994), which enhances the ombudsman's power, will significantly alter this pattern remains to be seen.

While parties and state bureaucracies have legitimized some women's concerns, they have undermined any demand or possibility for more radical change (Eduards 1986). The results of this study reveal the elitist aspects of the corporatist state. For those (i.e., men) with institutionalized access, innovation is facilitated and effective. For those without institutionalized access, innovation is far more difficult to achieve. For these reasons, one should not expect the Swedish state to depart radically from its current, disconcerting response to the plight of battered, raped, and sexually harassed women.

The United States

The American state adopted more extensive gender-specific reforms earlier and implemented them more effectively. This did not happen because America's state officials had a greater commitment to gender equality than their Swedish counterparts. It happened because federalism provided a scaffolding within which a powerful autonomous women's movement could grow and effectively insist that the state more rigorously pursue innovative policies beneficial to women.

The weakness and decentralized structure of the American state legitimizes a proliferation of independent, diverse political movements. The women's movement offers a case in point. The state lacks both the capacity to integrate such interests and the authority to restrain them significantly. Consequently, American feminists are able to approach reform unfettered by the political establishment.

By withholding their allegiance from the two major political parties, American feminists tend to support only those individual candidates and state officials most firmly committed to their particular issues. American feminists are not constrained by the discipline required in Swedish-style party politics. They exercise their options and initiate policies through a variety of other avenues: courts, voter-initiated referenda, civic associations, human rights commissions, congressional committees, state legislatures, and public protests. In fact, when well organized, the movement can be rather effective.

The position of American feminists vis-à-vis the state differs significantly from that of feminists in Sweden. In Sweden, activists (e.g., shelter activists) were entirely dependent on the state for program funding, data, and political support. American women were more self-reliant. In order to maintain their complete (fiscal) independence from the state some projects refused to accept any government funding; most, however, simply refused to rely exclusively on the state for support and, in general, funding for American projects was diversified. In addition, American feminists had more available avenues through which they could pursue their claims and grievances. They utilized courts, legislatures, and state and local human rights commissions and sometimes appealed directly to state agencies to implement administrative reforms. Given their relative freedom from particular parties, bureaucracies, and state funding, American women were in a less vulnerable position vis-à-vis the state. They therefore were encouraged to take risks, test new approaches, and demand more of the state.

American reforms were drafted by activists who had greater knowledge of the particular obstacles faced by abused women. Since initiatives for reform originated within an autonomous feminist movement, women could better dictate their substance. Consequently, while Swedish reforms suggested increased police response, American laws mandated it. Furthermore, American programs and services for raped and battered women are more likely to be run by activists committed to social change than by agency professionals whose goals are more therapeutic. The weak state offers more-diversified participation as well as a devolution of authority. This has worked to the benefit of American women, insofar as reforms were initiated by those who stood to profit most from them. Lastly, the American context inspired more extensive, original research on battering, rape, and sexual harassment than the Swedish.

The American state does not dominate public discourse, particularly as it pertains to women's abuse. American activists, therefore, maintain their own distinctive voice as women and use this to legitimize their own perceptions of the abuses they suffer. As a result, the politics that result from their insights and efforts are under their own authority. For this reason, American women have a greater potential to radically alter patriarchy.

Closing Thoughts

The laws and services available to physically and sexually abused women in Sweden lead to a discouraging view of centralized policy formation. In the United States, reform efforts and resultant policies have been dispersed at the state and local level, while Swedish reforms have been pursued and adopted only at the national level. The relative lack of local initiatives in the development and implementation of policies and programs for women should not be regarded as unusual within Sweden, because social reforms almost always are adopted at the national level. This could have positive effects, in that, once a favorable reform is adopted, the entire country must abide by it. But, as in the United States, the national level of Swedish policy development is generally impermeable to women's gender-specific requests.

At the national level, the United States, like Sweden, has proven resistant to the gender-specific requests of women. Nonetheless, its federalist structure encourages the development of more innovative policies and programs at the local level. Within federalism, interest groups move "from one level of government to another in an attempt to find the level at which they might try most advantageously to get what they want" (Schattsneider 1975, 10). Women in the United States have done just that. Whether through state or local assemblies, the courts, or referenda, they have pursued, implemented, and monitored reforms, adjusting them in response to experience, and will continue to do so.

All policies have their own patterns of politics. This study suggests that feminist issues are best resolved through the politics of pluralism within fragmented states. Such states are more permeable and effective in the passage and implementation of rules that specifically benefit women as a group. The more decentralized the state, the greater the likelihood that women can obtain regulatory policies that encourage a redistribution of power between the sexes.

It is difficult to discuss Sweden in a manner that defies the prevailing respect and often reverence accorded to this state. With 41 percent of all parliamentary seats held by women after the 1994 election, Sweden now has the highest percentage of women in parliament of any nation in the world. The United States, by comparison, has only 11 percent of women in the House and a mere 7 percent in the Senate. This condition prompted a *New York Times* editorial that praised the Swedes for setting a "high standard for sexual equality in politics" and characterized the United States as a state that has "left women badly represented in political life" (27 September 1994). So impoverished is our general understanding of "political life" that, even in the United States, where such life is more flexible, political mobilization outside the conventions of parties is often dismissed by political commentators as insignificant.

That American women constitute a smaller percentage of professional politicians means neither that women are not politically engaged in the United States nor that they are prevented from becoming so. Indeed, only weeks before the Swedish election, the National Women's Political Caucus in Washington released a study that found that "when women [in the United States] run for office, they win ... as often as men do" (Newman 1994).

Sweden's reputation is bolstered by those who continue to insist that political activity is measured primarily through party rosters. Political success, however, cannot be mechanically appraised by simplistic numbers. An examination of *sexual politics* in Sweden makes this clear. Including women in political parties does not necessarily mean that feminism flourishes.

Favorable, though inaccurate, information on Sweden is constantly published, often in reputable newspapers, journals, and books. A recent example concerns an article published in the *New York Times*. In "Sweden Redefines Sexual Revolution," reporter William Schmidt exclaims, "The sex clubs are gone, replaced by shops selling shoes and clothing.... [T]he only sex a foreign tourist will find advertised these days is in the form of telephone services" (22 March 1992). The only way to account for this thoroughly misguided conclusion is that, in the absence of zoning laws, pornography shops and "red light districts" are so well integrated into Swedish neighborhoods that they sometimes escape the notice of the untrained, foreign observer.

In a similar vein, books often contain references to battered women's shelters and/or rape crisis centers that do not exist. For example, in an otherwise informative study of Western European feminism, the author asserts that: "Today, all major cities in Sweden have refuges and rape crisis centres" (Kaplan 1992, 72).[6] One can

6. In Sweden, "jourer," meaning shelter, is the term used to describe crisis lines *and* actual shelters. In Swedish, there is no difference. And, as was mentioned in Chapters 3 and 4, these "jourer" perform several functions—sometimes including

account for this mistake and those like it only by realizing that few foreign scholars know Swedish and thus rely on English summaries of government commission reports and reprints provided by the Swedish Information Service. While government reports and the Swedish Information Service reprints are an invaluable resource for those wishing to know more about Sweden, these official state sources cannot be exclusively relied on to offer a broadened and more critical perspective on Sweden. Scholars and journalists should know this. The fact that we often do not suggests that we want there to be a state that is as nearly utopian as the Swedish state asserts itself to be. Indeed, we want that so desperately that we are unlikely to critically reflect upon those texts that conform to the vision of Sweden as we want it to be.

No state, however, is beyond reproach. While no state has managed to eradicate women's sexual subordination, some have been more willing than others to alleviate it. This fact is consistently ignored in more theoretical discussions concerning women and the state. The significance of the present study is not limited to its evaluation of which state structure has best fulfilled its obligation to provide for the physical well-being and psychological integrity of its female inhabitants, although this, itself, would have been important. It highlights the ability of feminist policies to inform state-centered discourse more generally. It provides a first step toward adopting a new direction in the study of women in particular and the state in general. It exposes the important role the state can have in the relief and prevention of human misery.

Feminist discussions of how best to confront misogyny have been linked increasingly to the question of whether the state can ever be instrumental in obtaining feminist objectives. Some insist that the state is hopelessly patriarchal and that feminists who demand that it be engaged to provide women assistance and relief are wasting their time (Smart 1989). However, within patriarchy, as within all oppressive situations, change must begin somewhere. The struggle for women's freedom is different from other political movements because, as Adrienne Rich reminds us, there is no place that is "no man's land." If one views the state as impermeable to feminist reforms, any meaningful resistance to male domination risks becoming insignificant, if not nonexistent (Elman 1989; MacKinnon 1989). The state is of interest not only because of its centrality

---

peripheral services that relate to rape crisis counseling. Uppsala University Hospital now provides a clinic for abused women; however, to date, there are no independent rape crisis centers in Sweden.

in maintaining patriarchy but, equally important, because of its structural susceptibility to change.

My findings suggest that a centralized state is better able to maintain the status quo, whether more or less equitable. While often depicted as wholly inadequate to administer change, the decentralized state emerges as more permeable to demands from those who wish to alter existing power relations. This permeability has also enhanced the state's effectiveness in implementing the reforms it has chosen to adopt. After all, the decentralized state is not only permeable to requests to adopt reforms; it is also accessible to those who wish to monitor reforms closely and seek to improve them. Unfortunately, however, the fragmented state may be just as permeable to requests from those who oppose feminist and progressive reforms.[7]

All patriarchal states are not identical in their approach to women's subordination. Only when we can recognize this can we appreciate the differences between states and select the appropriate strategies that work best in reducing inequality. This discussion suggests a more complex, even more subtle, relationship between state structure and reform than has previously been assumed by scholars of the state. It also reveals that no political victories can be taken for granted; whether as a guarantor of equity or as an object of resistance to demands for equity, the state can not be counted on to provide women with justice. Women, therefore, must be vigilant in making the state consistently responsive to their demands.

---

7. One could argue that this is precisely what happened to American feminists who had worked hard to obtain safe and legal abortion for women. After the 1973 Supreme Court decision that granted abortion rights, activists grew complacent. Their sense of accomplishment led them to disregard the incremental inroads their opposition was making. Consequently, women lost considerable ground in the 1980s. It took nearly a decade for feminists to mobilize effectively to maintain their right to abortion. One could argue that such mobilization contributed significantly to Clinton's presidential victory in 1992.

REFERENCES

A Southern Women's Writing Collective. 1990. "Sex Resistance in Heterosexual Arrangements." In *The Sexual Liberals and the Attack on Feminism*, edited by Dorchen Leidholdt and Janice G. Raymond, 140–147. New York: Pergamon.
Adams, Carolyn Teich, and Kathryn Teich Winston. 1980. *Mothers at Work: Public Policies in the United States, Sweden and China*. New York: Longman.
Agebjörn, Annika, and Birgitta Hellman. 1988. "Våldtagna kvinnor är rättslösa" [Raped women are without justice]. *Aftonbladet*, 19 January.
Allardt, Erik. 1986. "Representative Government in a Bureaucratic Age." In *Norden—The Passion for Equality*, edited by Stephen Graubard, 200–225. Oslo: Norwegian University.
Allen, Judith. 1990. "Does Feminism Need a Theory of 'The State'?" In *Playing the State: Australian Feminist Interventions*, edited by Sophie Watson, 21–37. New York: Verso.
Andersen, Bent Rold. 1984. "Rationality and Irrationality of the Nordic Welfare State." *Daedalus* 113(Winter): 109–139.
Anton, Thomas J. 1969. "Policy Making and Political Culture in Sweden." *Scandinavian Political Studies* 4: 88–102.
———. 1980. *Administered Politics: Elite Political Cultures in Sweden*. Boston: Martinus Nighoff.
Arendt, Hannah. 1970. *On Violence*. New York: A Harvest-HBJ Book.
Attorney General's Task Force. 1984. *Report on Family Violence: Final Report*. Washington, D.C.: Department of Justice (September).
Baehr, Ninia. 1990. *Abortion Without Apology: A Radical History for the 1990's*. Boston: South End.
Barnes v. Costle, 561 F2d 983 (D.C. Cir. 1977).
Barry, Kathleen. 1979. *Female Sexual Slavery*. Englewood Cliffs, New Jersey: Prentice Hall.
Bart, Pauline, and, Patricia O'Brien. 1985. *Stopping Rape: Successful Survival Strategies*. New York: Pergamon.
Becker, Mary, Cynthia Grant Bowman, and Morrison Torrey. 1994. *Feminist Jurisprudence: Taking Women Seriously*. St. Paul: West.
Bennett-Alexander, Dawn D. 1991. "Lower Court Interpretation of the Meritor Decision: Putting Flesh on the Supreme Court's Sexual Harassment Skeleton." *Wisconsin Women's Law Journal* 6: 35–85.
Bergman, Bo. 1987. *Battered Wives: Why Are They Beaten and Why Do They Stay?* Stockholm: Repro Print AB.
Bienen, Leigh. 1983. "Rape Reform Legislation in the United States: A Look at Some Practical Effects." *Victimology* 8 (1–2): 139–151.

Swedish readers will note that the alphabetization has been Anglicized.

Bodström, Cecilia. 1989. "Hon vågade säga emot sin sambo" [She dared to speak out against her man]. *Expressen*, 12 April.
Boëthius, Maria-Pia. 1976. *Skylla sig själv: En bok om våldtäkt* [Blame yourself: A book about rape]. Stockholm: Liber Förlag.
———. 1989. "Våldtagna är rättslösa" [The raped are without justice]. *Dagens Nyheter*, 21 May.
———. 1990. *Patriarkatets våldsamma sammanbrott & Varför våldtäkt finns* [Patriarchy's violent collapse and why rape exists]. Stockholm: Bonniers.
Bohlen, Celestine. 1988. "Domestic Violence Arrests Quadruple in New York." *New York Times*, 28 December.
Borchorst, Anette, and Birte Siim. 1987. "Women and the advanced welfare state— a new kind of patriarchal power?" In *Women and the State*, edited by Anne Showstack Sassoon, 128–157. London: Hutchinson.
Borgblad, Margareta. 1992. *Sexuella trakasserier på Stockholms universitet* [Sexual harassment at Stockholm University]. Stockholm: Stockholms universitet.
BRÅ. 1983:4. *Utlänningarna och brottsligheten* [Foreigners and Criminality]. Stockholm: National Council for Crime Prevention.
———. 1984:1. *Den svenska våldsbrottsligheten* [Crimes of Violence in Sweden]. Stockholm: Report issued from the National Council for Crime Prevention.
BRÅ, PM. 1989:2. "Lagen om besöksförbud: En uppföljning" [The law concerning orders of protection: An investigation of their implementation]. Government Memorandum. Stockholm: The National Council for Crime Prevention.
Bradley v. State, 158, Miss. 1824.
Brännström, Leif. 1990. "Polisen tror inte på våldtäkten i hissen" [The police disbelieve rape in the elevator]. *Expressen*, 7 November.

Bravo, Ellen, and Ellen Cassedy. 1992. *The 9 to 5 Guide to Combatting Sexual Harassment: Candid Advice from 9 to 5, the National Association of Working Women*. New York: John Wiley.
Brodyaga Lisa, Margaret Gates, et al. 1975. *Rape and Its Victims: A Report for Citizens, Health Facilities, and Criminal Justice Agencies*. Washington, D. C.: National Institute for Law Enforcement and Criminal Justice, Law Enforcement Assistance Administration, Department of Justice.
Broman, Stellan. 1988. Interview by author. Central Prosecutors' Office, Stockholm, 25 August.
Brown, Wendy. 1992. "Finding the Man in the State." *Feminist Studies* 18(1): 7–34.
Brownmiller, Susan. 1976. *Against Our Will*. New York: Bantam.
Bruno v. Codd, 396 N.Y.S.2d, 974 (1977).
Burt, Martha, Janet C. Gornick, and Karen Pittman. 1984. *Feminism and Rape Crisis Centers*. Washington, D.C.: The Urban Institute.
Butler, Twiss. 1990. "Abortion and Pornography: The Liberals' 'Gotcha' Against Women's Equality." In *The Sexual Liberals and the Attack on Feminism*, edited by Dorchen Leidholdt and Janice G. Raymond, 114–122. New York: Pergamon.
Canton Ohio v. Harris, U.S. 489 378 (1989).
Caputi, Jane. 1987. *Age of the Sex Crime*. Bowling Green, Ohio: Bowling Green University Popular.
Carlstedt, Gunilla. 1992. *Kvinnors hälsa: En fråga om makt* [Women's health: A question of power]. Stockholm: Tiden/Folksam.
Carnoy, Martin. 1984. *The State & Political Theory*. Princeton: Princeton University.

Celis, William. 1991. "Students Draw Line Between Sex and an Assault." *New York Times*, 2 January.
Center for Women and Policy Studies. 1975. *Community Anti-Rape Projects*. Washington, D.C.: Center for Women and Policy Studies.
Chamallas, Martha. 1992. "Feminist Constructions of Objectivity: Multiple Perspectives in Sexual and Racial Litigation." *Texas Journal of Women and the Law* 1: 95–142.
Chapman, Jane Roberts, and Gordon R. Chapman. 1984a. "Sexual Harassment of Women in Employment, Part II: Legal Remedies." *Response* 7(3): 3–4, 12.
———. 1984b. "Sexual Harassment of Women in Employment, Part III: Promising Solutions." *Response* 7(4): 8–11.
Civil Rights Act, P.L. 102–166, 102d Cong., 2d Sess., 105 Stat. 1071, 1991.
Civildepartementet. 1989. "Utdrag ur protokoll vid regeringssammanträde 1989-11-23, Jä 2579/89, jämte bilaga." [Excerpts from government proceedings]. Stockholm.
———. 1991. *Om våld mot kvinnor—en rapport från arbetsgruppen för frågor om våld mot kvinnor* [On violence against women—A report from the working group for questions concerning violence against women]. Stockholm: Government Report.
Collins, Patricia Hill. 1993. "The Sexual Politics of Black Womanhood." In *Violence Against Women: The Bloody Footprints*, edited by Pauline Bart and Eileen Moran, 85–104. London: Sage.
Connell, Noreen, and Cassandra Wilson. 1974. *Rape: The First Sourcebook for Women*. New York: Plume.
Coontz, Stephanie. 1992. *The Way We Never Were: American Families and the Nostalgia Trap*. New York: Basic.
Copeland, Lois. 1991. Telephone conversation with author. Center for Women and Policy Studies, Washington, D.C., 15 April.
Corne v. Bausch and Lomb, Inc., 390 F. Supp. 161 (D. Ariz. 1975).
Craib, Ralph. 1977. "Sex and Women at UC Berkeley—2 Surveys." *The San Francisco Chronicle*, 22 July.
Crenshaw, Kimberlè Williams. 1992. "Whose Story Is It, Anyway? Feminist and Antiracist Appropriations of Anita Hill." In *Race-ing Justice, En-gendering Power: Essays on Anita Hill, Clarence Thomas, and the Construction of Social Reality*, edited by Toni Morrison, 402–440. New York: Pantheon.
———. 1993. "Beyond Racism and Misogyny: Black Feminism and 2 Live Crew." In *Words That Wound: Critical Race Theory, Assaultive Speech, and the First Amendment*, Mari J. Matsuda, Charles R. Lawrence III, Richard Delgado, and Kimberlè Williams Crenshaw, 111–132. Boulder: Westview.
Dagens Nyheter. 1992. "Allt fler kvinnor söker hjälp" [More and more women seek help]. 29 May.
Dahl, Hans F. 1986. "Those Equal Folk." In *Norden—The Passion for Equality*, edited by Stephen Graubard, 97–111. Oslo: Norwegian University.
Dahlberg, Anita, Gudrun Nordborg, and Elvy Wiklund. 1989. *Kvinnors rätt* [Women's rights]. Stockholm: Tiden/Folksam.
Dahlberg, Anita. 1993. Interview by author. Center for Research on Women, Stockholm, 21 January.
Dahlerup, Drude. 1987. "Confusing concepts—Confusing Reality: A Theoretical Discussion of the Patriarchal State." In *Women and the State*, edited by Anne Showstack Sassoon, 93–127. London: Hutchinson.

———. 1994. "Learning To Live With The State." *Women's Studies International Forum* 17(2/3): 117–127.
Danielson, Mona. 1988. Interview by author. Ministry of Labor, Stockholm, 26 August.
Daun, Åke. 1989. *Svensk mentalitet: ett jämförande perspektiv* [The Swedish mentality: A comparative perspective]. Stockholm: Raben & Sjögren.
Dinnerstein, Leonard. 1994. *Antisemitism in America*. Oxford: Oxford University.
Directive 1993:88, Committee Directives. *The Swedish Government Commission on Violence Against Women*. Stockholm: Ministry of Social Affairs.
Dobash, R. Emerson. 1990. "Shaping Gender Through Violence." Paper presented at the Swedish Council for Research in the Humanities and Social Sciences International Symposium, October.
Dobash, R. Emerson, and Russell P. Dobash. 1992. *Women, Violence and Social Change*. New York, Routledge.
Ds 1990:3. *Kartläggning av våldtäktsbrotten—analys av den aktuella situationen, förslag till åtgärder* [A survey of rape crimes—Analysis of the situation today and suggested measures]. Stockholm: Allmänna Förlaget.
Ds 1992:92. *Act concerning equality between men and women*. Stockholm: Allmänna Förlaget.
Ds Ju 1987:13. "Sammanställning av remissyttranden över departementspromemorian, Besöksförbud" [A summary of remiss regarding orders of protection]. Stockholm: Ministry of Justice.
DuBois, Ellen Carol. 1978. *Feminism and Suffrage: The Emergence of an Independent Women's Movement in America 1848–1869*. Ithaca, NY: Cornell University.
Duvander, Christina. 1983. "Allmänt åtal vid kvinnomisshandel" [Public prosecution of woman battery]. Unpublished legal essay, Department of Social Work, Stockholm University.
Edqvist, Björn, and Suzanne Wennberg. 1983. "Recent Legislation and Research on Victims in Sweden." *Victimology* 8(1–2): 310–327.
Eduards, Maud L. 1986. "Kön, stat och jämställdhetspolitik" [Sex, state and equality policies]. *Kvinnovetenskaplig tidskrift*, no. 3: 4–15.
———. 1988. "Gender Politics and Public Policies in Sweden." Paper presented at symposium, Women and Power: The Swedish Experience in Comparative Perspective. Harvard University Center for European Studies, Cambridge, MA, October.
———. 1989. "The Third Way: On Women's Politics and Welfare Policies in Sweden." Paper presented at symposium, Women, Power and Strategies for Change. The Swedish Institute, Stockholm, November.
———. 1992. "Against the Rules of the Game: On the Importance of Women's Collective Actions." In *Rethinking Change: Current Swedish Feminist Research*, edited by Maud L. Eduards, Eva Lundgren, and Ulla Wikander, 83–104. Uppsala: Swedish Science.
Ehrhart, Julie K., and Bernice R. Sandler. 1986. "Party Rape." *Response* 9(1): 2–5.
Eisenberg, Sue, and Patricia L. Micklow. 1977. "The Assaulted Wife: Catch 22 Revisited." *Women's Rights Law Reporter* 3: 138–160.
Ekselius, Eva. 1990. "Könet—vanmaktens vapen" [Sex—the weapon of powerlessness]. *Dagens Nyheter*, 28 November.
Elman, R. Amy. 1989. "Sexual Subordination and State Intervention: Lessons for Feminists from the Nazi State." *Trivia* 15(Fall): 50–64.
———. 1991. "Den svenska modellen" [The Swedish model]. In *Pornografi:Verklighet eller Fantasi?* [Pornography: Reality or Fantasy?], 36–44. Stockholm: Williamsons.

———, and Maud L. Eduards. 1991. "Unprotected by the Swedish Welfare State: A Survey of Battered Women and the Assistance They Received." *Women's Studies International Forum* 14(5): 413–421.
Elman, R. Amy. 1993a. "Debunking the Social Democrats and the Myth of Equality." *Women's Studies International Forum* 16(5): 513–522.
———. 1993b. "From Battery and Rape to Prostitution: Transformations in Consciousness." Lecture presented to the All Women's House, Stockholm, January.
Epstein, Steven. 1987. "New Connecticut Law on Domestic Violence." *Women's Advocate*, January.
Esping-Anderson, Gösta, Roger Freidland, and Erik O. Wright. 1976. "Modes of Class Struggle and the Capitalist State." *Kapitalistate* (4–5): 186–220.
Estrich, Susan. 1987. *Real Rape*. Cambridge: Harvard University.
———. 1991. "Sex At Work." *Stanford Law Review* 43(4): 813–861.
European, The. 1993. "Paternity Leave." 12–15 August.
Evans, Laura J. 1978. "Sexual Harassment: Women's Hidden Occupational Hazard." In *The Victimization of Women*, edited by Jane Roberts Chapman and Margaret Gates, 203–223. London: Sage.
Evans, Peter, Dietrich Rueschemeyer, and Theda Skocpol, eds. 1985. *Bringing The State Back In*. New York: Cambridge University.
Fälth, Gun. 1992. "Misshandlad kvinna kan få livvaktsskydd" [Battered woman can receive bodyguard]. *Dagens Nyheter*, 25 June.
———. 1994. "Våldtäktsmän ofta utslagna" [Rapist often an outcast]. *Dagens Nyheter*, 5 May.
Farley, Lin. 1978. *Sexual Shakedown*. New York: McGraw Hill.
Ferraro, Kathleen, J. 1989. "The Legal Response to Woman Battering in the United States." In *Women, Policing, and Male Violence: International Perspectives*, edited by Jalna Hanmer and Elizabeth Stanko 155–184. New York: Routledge.
———. 1993. "Cops, Courts, and Woman Battering." In *Violence Against Women: The Bloody Footprints*, edited by Pauline Bart and Eileen Moran, 165–192. London: Sage.
Finkelhor, David. 1981. Testimony and Statement to Judiciary Committee, New Hampshire State Legislature, March 25.
Fleming, Jennifer Baker. 1979. *Stopping Wife Abuse: A Guide to the Emotional, Psychological and Legal Implications for the Abused Woman and Those Helping*. New York: Anchor.
Forsberg, Ulla-Britt. 1988. Interview by author. The All Women's House, Stockholm, 11 August.
Forslund, Per-Olov. 1988. Interview by author. The Stockholm Police Department, Stockholm, 15 August.
———. 1993. Interview by author. The Stockholm Police Department, Stockholm, 19 January.
Foucault, Michel. 1978. *The History of Sexuality*. Vol. 1. New York: Random House.
Fox-Genovese, Elizabeth. 1991. *Feminism Without Illusions*. Chapel Hill, NC: University of North Carolina.
Från Riksdag & Departement. 1990:8. "Fel i massmedia om våldtäkter" [Mistake in the mass media regarding rapes]. Stockholm: Parliamentary report.
Franklin v. Gwinnett County Public Schools, 112 S. Ct 1028, 1992.
Freeman, Jo. 1975. *The Politics of Women's Liberation*. New York: McKay.
Freud, Sigmund. 1969. *Dora: An Analysis of a Case of Hysteria*. New York: Collier.

Friedman, Deb. 1981. "Professionalism." *Aegis: Magazine on Ending Violence Against Women* 31: 36–38.

Frieze, Irene Hanson. 1980. "Causes and consequences of marital rape." Paper presented at the annual meeting of the American Psychological Association, Montreal.

Frye, Marilyn. 1983. *The Politics of Reality: Essays in Feminist Theory.* New York: Crossing.

Gambon, Jill. 1989. "Sexual Tension." *The Boston Tab*, 2 May.

Geis, Gilbert. 1978. "Rape-in-Marriage: Law and Law Reform in England, The United States, and Sweden." *The Adelaide Law Review* 6(2): 284–303.

Gelb, Joyce. 1983. "The politics of wife abuse." In *Families, Politics and Public Policy*, edited by Irene Diamond, 250–262. New York: Longman.

———. 1987. "Swedish State Equality: Feminism without Feminists." Paper presented to the annual meeting of the American Political Science Association, September.

———. 1990. *Feminism and Politics: A Comparative Perspective*, Berkeley: University of California.

Gelles, Richard. 1972. *The Violent Home.* Beverly Hills, CA: Sage.

Giddings, Paula. 1985. *When and Where I Enter: The Impact of Race and Sex in America.* New York: Bantam.

Gilder, George. 1974. *Sexual Suicide.* London: Milington.

Goodman, Ellen. 1982. "Equal Rights Award." *The Boston Globe*, 25 August.

Gordon, Linda, ed. 1990. *Women, the State, and Welfare.* Madison, Wisconsin: University of Wisconsin.

Gornick, Janet C., Martha Burt, and Karen Pittman. 1983. *Structure and Activities of Rape Crisis Centers in the Early 1980's.* Washington, D.C.: The Urban Institute.

Grau, Janice, Jeffrey Fagan, and Sandra Wexler. 1984. "Restraining Orders for Battered Women: Issues of Access and Efficacy." *Women and Politics* 4(3): 13–28.

Griffin, Susan. 1986. *Rape: The Politics of Consciousness.* San Francisco: Harper.

Grimstad, Kristen, and Susan Rennie. 1973. *The New Woman's Survival Catalog.* New York: Coward, McCann and Geoghegan Berkley Publishing.

Gustafsson, Thomas. 1989. "Allt färre fälls i våldtäktsmål" [Fewer and fewer are convicted in rape Trials]. *Svenska Dagbladet*, 2 May.

Haavio-Mannila, Elina, Drude Dahlerup, et al., eds. 1985. *The Unfinished Democracy —Women in Nordic Politics.* New York: Pergamon.

Hagman, Ninni. 1988. *Sextrakasserier på jobbet: Myter–Fakta–Råd* [Sexual harassment at work: Myths–Facts–Advice]. Stockholm: Wahlström & Wistrand.

———. 1992a. "Fritt fram för sextrakasserier" [There is no stopping sexual harassers]. *Dagens Nyheter*, 17 January.

———. 1992b. "Measures Taken in Sweden to Combat Sexual Harassment at Work: Report to the International Labour Office (ILO)." Stockholm: Stockholm University, February.

Hamos, Julie. 1980. *State Domestic Violence Laws and How to Pass Them.* Monograph Series, No 2. Washington, D.C.: National Clearinghouse on Domestic Violence, June.

Harris v. Forklift Systems Inc., 114 S. Ct. 367, 1993.

Hartz, Louis. 1955. *The Liberal Tradition in America: An Interpretation of American Thought Since the Revolution.* New York: Harcourt, Brace & World.

Heclo, Hugh, and Henrik Madsen. 1987. *Policy and Politics in Sweden: Principled Pragmatism.* Philadelphia: Temple University.

Hedlund, Eva, and Gunilla Lundmark. 1983:1. *Våldtäkt—Vanmakt: 60 män berättar* [Rape—Powerlessness: 60 men tell their stories]. Stockholm: Delegation for Social Research, Rapport.

Hedlund, Eva, and Marianne Granö. 1988. Interview by author. RFSU (Sweden's National Association for Sex Education), Stockholm, 23 August.
Held, David. 1989. *Political Theory and the Modern State.* Stanford, CA: Stanford University.
———, ed. 1991. *Political Theory Today.* Stanford, CA: Stanford University.
Hernes, Gudmund, and Arne Selvik. 1981. "Local Corporatism." In *Organizing Interests in Western Europe: Pluralism, Corporatism, and the Transformation of Politics,* edited by Suzanne Berger, 103–119. Cambridge: Cambridge University.
Hernes, Helga Maria. 1988. "The Welfare State Citizenship of Scandinavian Women." In *The Political Interests of Gender,* edited by Kathleen B. Jones and Anna G. Jónasdóttir, 187–213. London: Sage.
Hirdman, Yvonne. 1994. "Women—From Possibility to Problem?: Gender Conflict in the Welfare State—The Swedish Model." *Research Report* 3. Stockholm: Swedish Center for Working Life.
Hirshman, Linda. 1994. "Making Safety A Civil Right." *Ms.*, September/October, 44–47.
Högsta Domstolens (HD) 1980:137 No. 34, 3 December, B 900/80.
Hole, Judith, and Ellen Levine. 1971. *Rebirth of Feminism.* New York: Quadrangle.
Hydén, Margareta. 1992. *Woman Battering as a Marital Act: The Construction of a Violent Marriage.* Stockholm: Academitryck.
Ingvardsson, Margo. 1989. Interview by author. Communist Party headquarters, Stockholm, 16 October.
Jahn, Carin. 1987. "Kvinnomisshandel—förmildrande omständigheter?" [Woman battery—Extenuating circumstances?]. Unpublished legal thesis, Stockholm University Law School.
JÄMO. 1987a. *FRID-A Projektet.* Summary Report from the Equality Ombudsman's Office, Stockholm.
JÄMO. 1987b. "JämO—rapporten om sexuella trakasserier mot kvinnor i arbetslivet" [The Ombudsman's report on sexual harassment against women at work]. *JÄMSIDES* (March): 3.
Jenson, Jane, Elisabeth Hagen, and Ceallaigh Reddy, eds. 1988. *Feminization of the Labour Force: Paradoxes and Promises.* Cambridge: Polity.
Johansson, Astrid. 1991. "Kvinnovåldet allt grövre" [Violence against women worsens]. *Dagens Nyheter,* 8 March.
Jónasdóttir, Anna G. 1988. "On the Concept of Interest, Women's Interests, and the Limitations of Interest Theory." In *The Political Interests of Gender,* edited by Kathleen B. Jones and Anna G. Jónasdóttir, 33–65. London: Sage.
Jonung Christina, and Bodil Thordarsson. 1980. "Sweden." In *Women Returning to Work: Policies and Progress in Five Countries,* edited by Alice M. Yohalem, 107–159. Montclaire, NJ: Landmark Studies, Allenheld and Osmon.
Joreen. 1973. "The Tyranny of Structurelessness." In *Radical Feminism,* edited by Anne Keodt, Ellen Levine, and Anita Rapone, 285–299. New York: Quadrangle.
Justitiedepartementet. 1991. *Misshandel och sexuella övergrepp mot kvinnor och barn* [Battery and sexual assault against women and children]. Stockholm: Allmänna Förlaget.
Kälveston, Anna-Lisa. 1965. *The Social Structure of Sweden.* Stockholm: Swedish Institute.
Kaplan, Gisela. 1992. *Contemporary Western European Feminism.* New York: New York University.
Kelman, Steven. 1981. *Regulating America/Regulating Sweden.* Cambridge, MA: MIT.

Kerpner, Joachim. 1990. "Bara en av 200 Misshandlade kvinnor får polisskydd" [Only one of 200 battered women receive police protection]. *Stockholm (TT)*, 24 July.

Kesselman, Mark. 1982. "Prospects for Democratic Socialism in Advanced Capitalism: Class Struggle and Compromise in Sweden and France." *Politics & Society* 11(4): 397–438.

Kram, Ebon. 1990. Interview by author. The National Organization of Emergency Shelters for Battered Women in Sweden, Stockholm, 16 October.

———. 1993. Interview by author. The National Organization of Emergency Shelters for Battered Women in Sweden, Stockholm, 8 January.

Krasner, Stephen D. 1978. *Defending the National Interest*. Princeton, NJ: Princeton University.

Kvinnobulletinen. 1987. "Manscentrum får samhällsstod" [Men's center receives state funds] (6): 32.

Landau, Reva. 1987. "Lesser Lives and Greater Misrepresentations. Review of *A Lesser Life: The Myth of Women's Liberation in America*," by Sylvia Ann Hewlett. *Feminist Issues*, Fall, 60–94.

Langelan, Martha J. 1993. *Back Off! How to Confront and Stop Sexual Harassment and Harassers*. New York: Fireside.

Largen, Mary Ann. 1981. "Grassroots Centers and National Task Forces: A Herstory of the Anti-Rape Movement." *Aegis: Magazine on Ending Violence Against Women*, Autumn, 46–52.

Lavelle, Marianne. 1989. "A System of Failure." *The National Law Journal*, 24 April.

Lavén, Håkan. 1988. Interview by author. Ministry of Justice, Stockholm, 24 August.

Leander, Karen. 1988. Interview by author. Sweden's Statistics Bureau, Stockholm, 25 August.

———. 1989. "Misshandlade kvinnors möte med rättsapparaten" [Battered women meet the criminal justice apparatus]. In *Kvinnomisshandel* 14, 41–59. Stockholm: Jämfo Rapport.

———. 1992. "Kvinnomisshandel och våldtäkt i kriminalstatistiken" [Woman battering and rape in the criminal statistics]. Paper presented to symposium, Att möta våld mot kvinnor [Confronting violence against women]. The Police Academy, October. Later published by the Police Academy, Stockholm.

Leghorn, Lisa, and Katherine Parker. 1981. *Woman's Worth*. London: Routledge & Kegan Paul.

LeGrand, Camille. 1973. "Rape and Rape Laws: Sexism in Society and Law." *California Law Review* 61: 919–941.

Lerman, Lisa G, and Franci Livingston. 1983. "State Legislation on Domestic Violence." *Response* 6(5): 1–5.

———. 1986. "Prosecution of Wife Beaters: Institutional Obstacles and Innovations." In *Violence in the Home: Interdisciplinary Perspectives*, edited by Mary Lystad, 250–295. New York: Brunner/Mazel.

Lewin, Tamar. 1991. "Nude Pictures Are Ruled Sexual Harassment." *New York Times*, 23 January.

Lindahl, Björn. 1990. "Återfallen vanliga bland våldtäktsmän" [Recidivism common among rapists]. *Dagens Nyheter*, 7 April.

Lindau, Rebecka. 1993. "A Sexualized Image of Lesbianism in Sweden." *off our backs*, June, 10.

Lipset, Seymour Martin. 1967. *The First New Nation*. New York: Doubleday.

Lowi, Theodore. 1979. *The End of Liberalism: The Second Republic of The United States*. New York: Norton.

Lundgren, Eva. 1992a. "The Hand that Strikes and Comforts: Gender Construction in the Field of Tension Encompassing Body and Symbol, Stability and Change." In *Rethinking Change: Current Swedish Feminist Research*, edited by Maud L. Eduards, Eva Lundgren, and Ulla Wikander, 131–158. Uppsala: Swedish Science.
———. 1992b. *Gud och alla andra karlar—En bok om kvinnomisshandlare* [God and all the other guys—A book about batterers]. Stockholm: Natur och Kultur.
Lundgren, Eva, and Kristin Eriksen. 1988. "Fördomsfullt om kvinnomisshandel" [Prejudices about women battering]. *Socialt Arbete*, April, 18–21.
Lynberg, Gunilla. 1988. Interview by author. Central Prosecutors' Office, Stockholm, 30 August.
MacKinnon, Catharine A. 1979. *Sexual Harassment of Working Women*. New Haven, CT: Yale University.
———. 1982. "Feminism, Marxism, Method and the State: An Agenda for Theory." *Signs* 7(3): 515–544.
———. 1983. "Feminism, Marxism, Method and the State: Toward Feminist Jurisprudence." *Signs* 8(4): 635–658.
———. 1987. *Feminism Unmodified: Discourses on Life and Law*. Cambridge, MA: Harvard University.
———. 1989. *Toward A Feminist Theory of the State*. Cambridge, MA: Harvard University.
———. 1991. "Reflections on Sex Equality Under Law." *The Yale Law Journal* 100: 1281–1328.
———. 1994. "Rape, Genocide, and Women's Human Rights." *Harvard Women's Law Journal* 17(Spring): 5–16.
Malmborg, Jan. 1989. "Våldtäktsutredning dröjer ett halvår" [Rape investigations wait a half year]. *Dagens Nyheter*, 26 July 26.
Marsh, Jeanne C., Alison Geist, and Nathan S. Caplan. 1982. *Rape and the Limits of Law Reform*. Boston: Auburn House.
Martin, Dell. 1976. *Battered Wives*. San Francisco, CA: Glide.
Matthews, Nancy A. 1993. "Surmounting a Legacy: The Expansion of Racial Diversity in a Local Anti-Rape Movement." In *Violence Against Women: The Bloody Footprints*, edited by Pauline Bart and Eileen Moran, 177–192. London: Sage.
———. 1994. *Confronting Rape: The Feminist Anti-Rape Movement and the State*. London: Routledge.
Mauss, Armand L. 1975. *Social Problems as Social Movements*. Philadelphia: J. B. Lippincott.
McDonald, N. 1976. "Consulting." *Feminist Alliance Against Rape* 3 (Spring): 6–7.
Mehrhof, Barbara, and Pamela Kearon. 1973. "Rape: An Act of Terror." In *Radical Feminism*, edited by Anne Keodt, Ellen Levine, and Anita Rapone, 228–233. New York: Quadrangle.
Meritor Savings Bank v. Vinson, 477 U.S. 57, 68 (1986).
Miliband, Ralph. 1969. *The State in Capitalist Society*. New York: Basic.
Miller v. Bank of America, 418 F. Supp. 233 (N. D. Cal. 1976).
Millett, Kate. 1970. *Sexual Politics*. New York: Avon.
Milloy, Ross E. 1992. "Furor Over a Decision Not to Indict a Rape Case." *New York Times*, 25 October.
Milner, Henry. 1989. *Sweden: Social Democracy in Practice*. London: Oxford University.
Ministry of Foreign Affairs. 1991. "Racist Upsurge." *Sweden Report* 2 (December).
Mitchell, Timothy P. 1991. "The Limits of the State: Beyond Statist Approaches and Their Critics." *American Political Science Review* 85(1): 77–96.

———. 1992. "Going Beyond the State." *American Political Science Review* 86(4): 1017–1020.

Morgan, Robin. 1984. *Sisterhood is Global*. New York: Anchor.

Morone, James A. 1990. *The Democratic Wish: Popular Participation and the Limits of American Government*. New York: Basic.

Morrison, Toni, ed. 1992. *Race-ing Justice, En-gendering Power: Essays on Anita Hill, Clarence Thomas, and the Construction of Social Reality*. New York: Pantheon.

Motion 1981/1982: 874.

Motion 1982/1983: 314.

Motion 1982/1983: 685.

Motion 1983/1984: 2177.

Ms.. 1992. Letters. January/February, 8–11.

———. 1994. "No More! Stopping Domestic Violence." September/October, 33–65.

Mullins, D. 1983. "The Civil Suit: An Alternative for Rape Victims." *Response* 6(4): 3.

National Center for Women and Family Law. 1988. "Marital Rape Exemption Packet." New York: National Center for Women and Family Law, Inc.

National Coalition Against Domestic Violence. Undated. "Every 15 Seconds a Woman is Battered in This Country" (brochure). Denver: National Coalition Against Domestic Violence.

National Council for Crime Prevention. 1984:1. "Summaries of Reports: Crimes of Violence in Sweden." Stockholm: SCB.

Naumann, Cilla. 1988. "Ersättning till offren kan öka antalet brott" [Compensation for victims may increase the number of crimes reported]. *Dagens Nyheter*, 5 March.

Nemy, Enid. 1975. "Women Begin to Speak Out against Sexual Harassment." *New York Times*, 19 August.

New York Times. 1987. "Judges in Massachusetts Studying Spouse Abuse." 3 May.

———. 1988. "Court Reinstates a Woman's Suit Charging That Police Failed Her." 25 August.

———. 1991. "Rape Case: Badge vs. Badge." 10 April.

———. 1994. "A Parliament That Looks Like Sweden." Editorial, 27 September.

Newman, Judy. 1994. *Perception and Reality: A Study Comparing the Success of Men & Women Candidates*. Washington: National Women's Political Caucus.

Nilén, Holger. 1986. "Våldtäktsmannen—ett förvirrat barn" [The rapist—a confused child]. *Svenska Dagbladet*, 23 July.

Norris, Pippa. 1987. *Politics and Sexual Equality: The Comparative Position of Women in Western Democracies*, Boulder, CO: Riener.

Nycander, Svante. 1993. "Nyfeminismens vilsna tankar" [New Feminism's confused thoughts]. *Dagens Nyheter*, 31 January.

Oakley, Ann. 1981. "Interviewing Women: A Contradiction in Terms." In *Doing Feminist Research*, edited by Helen Roberts, 30–61. London: Routledge & Kegan Paul.

O'Connor, James. 1973. *The Fiscal Crisis of the State*. New York: St. Martins.

Önfelt, Cecilia. 1988. Interview by author. Center Party headquarters, Stockholm, 18 August.

Orloff, Ann Shola. 1988. "The Political Origins of America's Belated Welfare State." In *The Politics of Social Policy in the United States*, edited by Margaret Weir, Ann Shola Orloff, and Theda Skocpol, 37–80. Princeton, NJ: Princeton University.

O'Sullivan, Elizabethann. 1978. "What Has Happened to Rape Crisis Centers? A Look at Their Structures, Members and Funding." *Victimology* 3(1–2): 45–62.

Pateman, Carole. 1988a. *The Sexual Contract*. London: Polity.

———. 1988b. "The Patriarchal Welfare State." In *Democracy and the Welfare State*, edited by Amy Gutmann, 231–260. Princeton, NJ: Princeton University.
Pendo, Elizabeth. 1994. "Recognizing Violence Against Women: Gender and the Hate Crimes Statistics Act." *Harvard Women's Law Journal* 17(Spring): 157–183.
Peterson, Eric. 1977. "Interest Group Incorporation in Sweden." Paper presented to the annual meeting of the American Political Science Association, September.
Pittman, Karen, Martha Burt, and Karen Gornick. 1984. *The Internal Dynamics of Rape Crisis Centers*. Washington, D.C.: The Urban Institute.
Piven, Francis Fox, and Cloward, Richard A. 1971. *Regulating the Poor*. New York: Vintage.
———. 1977. *Poor People's Movements: Why They Succeed, How They Fail*. New York: Pantheon.
Pleck, Elizabeth. 1987. *Domestic Tyranny*. Oxford: Oxford University.
Poulantzas, Nicos. 1978. *Political Power and Social Classes*. London: Verso.
Premfors, Rune. 1983. "Governmental Commissions in Sweden." *American Behavioral Scientist* 26(5): 623–642.
Pringle, Rosemary, and Sophie Watson. 1990. "Fathers, Brothers, Mates: The Fraternal State in Australia." In *Playing the State: Australian Feminist Interventions*, edited by Sophie Watson, 229–243. New York: Verso.
Przeworski, Adam. 1989. *Capitalism and Social Democracy*. New York: Cambridge University.
Qwist, Gunilla. 1988. Interview by author. Prosecutors' Office, Stockholm, 15 August.
Radford, Jill, and Diana E. H. Russell, eds. 1992. *Femicide: The Politics of Woman Killing*. New York: Twayne.
Redbook. 1976. "How Do You Handle Sex on the Job: A Redbook Questionnaire." (January): 74–75.
Regeringens proposition 1989/1990: 158, 31 May, 1990.
Response. 1984. "Sexual Assault: The Facts." 7(2): 9–10.
Rhode, Deborah. 1989. *Justice and Gender: Sex Discrimination and the Law*. Cambridge, MA: Harvard University.
Rich, Adrienne. 1979. *On Lies, Secrets and Silence*. New York: Norton.
Rickenberg, M., and J. Shulman. 1984. "Florida, New York and Virginia Courts Declare Marital Rape a Crime." *Clearinghouse Review No. 18* (November): 745–750.
Riksorganisationen för kvinnojourer i Sverige (ROKS). 1990. Annual meeting of the National Organization of Emergency Shelters for Battered Women in Sweden, Kalmar, Sweden, 25 May.
Robinson v. Jacksonville Shipyards, Inc., 1991.
Rose, Vicky McNickle. 1977. "Rape as a Social Problem: A Byproduct of the Feminist Movement." *Social Problems* 25(1): 75–89.
Ruggie, Mary. 1984. *The State & Working Women: A Comparative Study of Britain and Sweden*. Princeton, NJ: Princeton University.
———. 1987. "Women's Movements and Women's Interests: The Impact of Labor State Relations in Britain and Sweden." In *The Women's Movements of the United States and Western Europe: Consciousness, Political Opportunity and Public Policy*, edited by Mary Fainsod Katzenstein and Carol M. Mueller, 247–266. Philadelphia: Temple University.

Ruin, Olof. 1982. "Sweden in the 1970's: Policy Making Becomes More Difficult." In *Policy Styles in Western Europe*, edited by Jeremy Richardson, 141–167. London: George Allen and Unwin.
Russell, Diana E. H. 1982. *Rape in Marriage*, New York: Macmillan.
———. 1984. *Sexual Exploitation*, New York: Macmillan.
Sainsbury, Diane. 1988. "The Scandinavian Model and Women's Interests: The Issues of Universalism and Corporatism." *Scandinavian Political Studies* 2(4): 337–346.
Salholz, Eloise, Lucille Beachy, et al. 1992. "Did America 'Get It'?" *Newsweek*, 28 December.
SANEnews. 1986. "Responses to the Attorney General's Task Force on Family Violence." February.
Sapiro, Virginia. 1986. "The Gender Basis of American Social Policy." *Political Science Quarterly* 2: 221–238.
Sarnecki, Jerzy. 1990. "Våldet—i massmedierna och verkligheten" [Rape—in the mass media and in reality]. *Dagens Nyheter*, 11 February.
Sassoon, Anne Showstack, ed. 1987. *Women and the State*. London: Hutchinson.
Schattschneider, Elmer Eric. 1975. *The Semisovereign People: A Realists View of Democracy in America*. Hinsdale, Illinois: Dryden.
Schechter, Susan. 1982. *Women and Male Violence: The Visions and Struggles of the Battered Women's Movement*: Boston: South End.
———. 1988. "Building Bridges Between Activists, Professionals, and Researchers." In *Feminist Perspectives on Wife Abuse*, edited by Kersti Yllö and Michele Bograd, 299–312. Newbury Park, CA: Sage.
Schirmer, Jennifer G. 1982. *The Limits of Reform: Women, Capital and Welfare*. Cambridge, MA: Schenkman.
Schmidt, Manfred G. 1982. "Does Corporatism Matter? Economic Crisis, Politics and Rates of Unemployment in Capitalist Democracies in the 1970s." In *Patterns of Corporatist Policy Making*, edited by Gerhard Lehmbruch and Philippe C. Schmitter, 237–258. Beverly Hills, CA: Sage.
Schmidt, William E. 1992. "Sweden Redefines Sexual Revolution." *New York Times*, 22 March.
Schmitt, Eric. 1989. "Family Violence: Protection Improves but Not Prevention." *New York Times*, 17 January.
Schmitter, Philippe C. 1974. "Still the Century of Corporatism?" *The Review of Politics* 36(1): 85–131.
———. 1982. "Reflections on Where the Theory of Neo-Corporatism Has Gone and Where the Praxis of Neo-Corporatism May Be Going." In *Patterns of Corporatist Policy Making*, edited by Gerhard Lehmbruch and Philippe C. Schmitter, 259–279. Beverly Hills, CA: Sage.
———. 1985. "Neocorporatism and the State." In *The Political Economy of Corporatism*, edited by Wyn Grant, 32–62. London: Macmillan.
Scott v. Hart, NoC–76–2395 (N.D. Cal., filed October 28, 1976).
Scott, Hilda. 1982. *Sweden's "Right to Be Human."* New York: Sharpe.
Scott, Joan. 1988. *Gender and The Politics of History*. New York: Columbia University.
Scott, Sara, and Alison Dickens. 1988. "Controlling with Kindness." *Trouble and Strife 13* (Spring): 40–45.
Scully, Diana, and Joseph Marolla. 1993. "'Riding the Bull at Gilley's': Convicted Rapists Describe the Rewards of Rape." In *Violence Against Women: The Bloody Footprints*, edited by Pauline Bart and Eileen Moran, 26–46. London: Sage.

References

SFS 1988: 688 *Lag om besöksförbud.*
SFS 1989: 1075. *Lag om besöksförbud.*
Sherman, Lawrence, and Richard A. Berk. 1984. "The Specific Deterrent Effects of Arrest for Domestic Assault." *American Sociological Review* 49: 261–272.
Side by Side: A Report on Equality Between Men and Women in Sweden 1985. 1985. Stockholm: Liber Förlag.
Sidel, Ruth. 1986. *Women and Children Last: The Plight of Poor Women in Affluent America.* New York: Penguin.
Skard, Torild, and Elina Haavio-Mannila. 1986. "Equality Between the Sexes— Myth or Reality in Norden?" In *Norden: The Passion for Equality,* edited by Stephen Graubard, 176–199. Oslo: Norwegian University.
Skocpol, Theda. 1985. "Bringing the State Back In: Strategies of Analysis in Current Research." In *Bringing The State Back in,* edited by Peter Evans, Dietrich Rueschemeyer, and Theda Skocpol, 3–37. New York: Cambridge University.
Smart, Carol. 1989. *Feminism and the Power of Law.* New York: Routledge.
Socialstyrelsen. 1985. *Misshandel och sexuella övergrepp mot kvinnor och barn.* [Battery and sexual assault against women and children]. Stockholm: Liber Förlag.
Soto v. County of Sacramento, N332313 Cal. Super. Ct., (January 8, 1986).
SOU 1976:9. *Sexuella övergrepp* [Sexual assault]. Stockholm: Liber Förlag.
SOU 1979:56. *Steg på väg—nationell handlingsplan för jämställdhet* [On the way— national action plan for equality]. Stockholm: Liber Förlag.
SOU 1982:61. *Våldtäkt och andra sexuella övergrepp* [Rape and other sexual assault]. Stockholm: Liber Förlag.
SOU 1986:49. *Målsägandebiträde* [Legal aid]. Stockholm: Liber Förlag.
SOU 1990:41. *Tio år med jämställdhetslagen—utvärdering och förslag* [Ten years with the equality act—evaluation and suggestions]. Stockholm: Liber Förlag.
SOU 1990:92. *Våld och brottsoffer* [Violence and crime victims]. Stockholm: Liber Förlag.
SOU 1994:56. *Ett centrum för kvinnor som våldtagits och misshandlats* [A center for raped and battered women]. Stockholm: Liber Förlag.
SOU 1995:60. *Kvinnofrid* [Women's Freedom from Male Violence]. Del A. Stockholm: Fritzes.
Spohn, Cassia, and Julie Horney. 1992. *Rape Law Reform: A Grass-Roots Revolution and Its Impact.* New York: Plenum.
Stanko, Elizabeth. 1985. *Intimate Intrusions: Women's Experience of Male Violence.* London: Routledge & Kegan Paul.
Stanley, Liz, and Sue Wise. 1993. *Breaking Out Again: Feminist Ontology and Epistemology.* London: Routledge & Kegan Paul.
State v. Oliver, 70, N.C., 60, 61, 1874.
Statistics Sweden. 1981. *Victims of Violence and Property Crimes #24.* Stockholm: SCB.
———. 1986. *Statistical Abstract of Sweden 1986.* Stockholm: SCB.
———. 1990. *Women and Men in Sweden: Equality of the Sexes 1990.* Stockholm: SCB.
———. 1991. *Statistiska meddelanden: Socialbidrag under 1991* [Statistical message: Social assistance during 1991]. Stockholm: SCB.
———. 1992. *On Women and Men in Sweden and the EC.* Stockholm: SCB.
Stenius, Yrsa. 1990. "Prostituerade mindre värda?" [Prostitutes, worth less?]. *Aftonbladet,* 15 December.
Stepan, Alfred. 1978. *The State and Society: Peru in Comparative Perspective.* Princeton, NJ: Princeton University.
Swedish Institute. 1993. "Equality between men and women in Sweden." *Fact Sheets on Sweden.* Stockholm.

Tagesson, Pelle. 1990. "Häktas inte för våldtäkt—offret var förlamat" [Man is not arrested for rape—the victim was paralysed]. *Expressen*, 24 March.
Thoreau, Henry. 1970. "On Civil Disobedience." In *The Portable Thoreau*, edited by Carl Bode, 109–137. New York: Viking.
Thunberg, Karin. 1990. "Vad säger statistiken egentligen?" [What do the statistics really say?]. *Svenska Dagbladet*, 25 April.
Tiby, Eva. 1987. "Kvinnor i nöd" [Women in Need]. *Kvinnobulletinen* 5: 24–25.
Tierney, Kathleen. 1982. "The Battered Women's Movement and the Creation of the Wife Beating Problem." *Social Problems* 29(3): 207–220.
Tocqueville, Alexis de. 1956. *Democracy in America*. New York: Mentor.
Tompkins v. New Jersey Public Service, Electric & Gas Company, 422 F. Supp. 533 (D. NJ. 1976).
Tong, Rosemarie. 1984. *Women, Sex and the Law*. New Jersey: Rowman & Allanheld.
Toufexis, Anastasia. 1987. "Home is Where the Hurt Is: Wife Beating among the Well-to-Do is No Longer a Secret." *Time*, 21 December.
U.S. Bureau of the Census. 1984. "Money and Income of Households, Families and Persons in the United States: 1984." *Current Population Reports* 151, Series P-60.
U.S. Commission on Civil Rights. 1982. *Under the Rule of Thumb: Battered Women and the Administration of Justice*. Washington, D.C.: Commission on Civil Rights.
U.S. Department of Justice. 1987. *Sexual Assault: An Overview*. Washington: Department of Justice, November.
U.S. Merit Systems Protection Board, Office of Merit Systems and Studies. 1981. *Sexual Harassment in the Federal Workplace: Is it a Problem?* Washington D.C: Government Printing Office.
U.S. President's Commission on Law Enforcement and the Administration of Justice. 1967. *Task Force Report: Crime and Its Impact —An Assessment*. Washington, D.C.: Government Printing Office.
Veblen, Thorstein. 1953. *The Theory of Leisure Class*. New York: Mentor.
Verba, Sidney, Steven Kelman, et al. 1987. *Elites and the Idea of Equality: A Comparison of Japan, Sweden and the United States*. Cambridge, MA: Harvard University.
Victimology. 1976. "Victimology Interview: The Washington D.C. Rape Crisis Center." 1(3): 434–445.
Vinciguerra, Marlisa. 1989. "The Aftermath of Meritor: A Search For Standards in the Law of Sexual Harassment." *The Yale Law Journal* 98: 1717–1738.
Wadstein, Margareta. 1988. Interview by author. Equality Ombudsman's Office, Stockholm, 8 August.
Walby, Sylvia. 1990. *Theorizing Patriarchy*. Cambridge: Basil Blackwell.
Warrior, Betsy. 1976. *Wife Beating*. Somerville, MA: New England Free Press.
———. 1985. *Battered Women's Directory*. Cambridge, MA: The Directory, 46 Pleasant Street.
Weber, Max. 1981. *From Max Weber: Essays in Sociology*. Translated and edited by Hans Henrich Gerth and C. Wright Mills. New York: Oxford University.
Weir, Margaret, Ann Shola Orloff, and Theda Skocpol, eds. 1988. *The Politics of Social Policy in the United States*. Princeton, NJ: Princeton University.
Williams, Linda. 1984. "The Classic Rape: When Do Victims Report?" *Social Problems* 31(4): 459–467.
Williams, Patricia J. 1991. *The Alchemy of Race and Rights: Diary of a Law Professor*. Cambridge, MA: Harvard University.
Wilson, Elizabeth. 1977. *Women and the Welfare State*. London: Tavistock.

Wilson, Graham K. 1982. "Why Is There No Corporatism in the United States?" In *Patterns of Corporatist Policy Making*, edited by Gerhard Lehmbruch and Philippe C. Schmitter, 218–236. Beverly Hills, CA: Sage.

Wistrand, Birgitta. 1981. *Swedish Women on the Move*. Stockholm: Swedish Institute.

Women's Advocate. 1989. Order of Protection Backlash. May.

Woods, Laurie. 1978. "Litigation on Behalf of Battered Women." *Women's Rights Law Reporter* 5(1): 1–34.

———. 1981. "Litigation on Behalf of Battered Women." *Women's Rights Law Reporter* 7(39): 39–45.

———. 1989. Interview by author. National Center on Women and Family Law, New York, 8 June.

Woolf, Virginia. 1966. *Three Guineas*. New York: Harcourt, Brace & World.

Working Women United Institute. 1975. "Sexual harassment on the job: Results of a preliminary survey." Unpublished paper. Ithaca, NY.

X, Laura. 1987. "Marital Rape: The Most Blatant Example of Women's Inequality." Public presentation. Berkeley: The National Clearinghouse on Marital Rape.

Yale Law Journal 81. 1972. "The Rape Corroboration Requirement." 7: 1365–1391.

Zetterberg, Hans L. 1986. "The Rational Humanitarians." In *Norden: The Passion for Equality*, edited by Stephen Graubard, 79–96. Oslo: Norwegian University.

INDEX

abolition, see United States, feminist movement, anti-slavery movement and
abortion, vii(n2), 9, 124(n7)
Acquired Immune Deficiency Syndrome (AIDS), 62, 79
Act on Equality Between Women and Men at Work (Sweden), see Equal Opportunities Act
All Women's House (Stockholm), 40, 41, 53, 59
Amnesty International, 50(n27)
analysis, class, 6, 9(n10), 11
analysis, feminist, viii(n4), ix-x; see also analysis, gender-specific
analysis, gender-neutral, 7–11, 77(n22), 115–116
analysis, gender-specific, vii–viii, x, 1–3, 7–13, 115–116
analysis, race, 11
analysis, state-centered, 1–3, 7; see also state structure
Anthony, Susan B., 18
anti-Semitism, 19(n2), 22(8)
Attorney General (U.S.), 47, 50

Barnes v. Costle, 101
battered woman shelters, 5(n6); see also Sweden, rape, shelters and; Sweden, woman battery, shelters; United States, woman battery, shelters
battery, see woman battery
Bible, 97(n9)
Biden, Sen. Joseph, 50
Boëthius, Maria-Pia, 71(n14)
BRÅ, see National Council for Crime Prevention (Sweden)

Bradley v. State, 43
Bremer, Fredrika, 17
Bruno v. Codd, 45
Bureau of Statistics (Sweden), 34, 74

Canton, Ohio v. Harris, 45(n18)
Carlsson, Prime Minister Ingvar, 56
cautionary instructions, 78, 80, 81, 86, 91
Center for Women Policy Studies (U.S.), 38
Center Party (Sweden), 52, 53, 54, 88
Child Abuse and Treatment Act (U.S.), 50
childcare programs, 9, 10, 95–96
Civil Rights Act (1964, U.S.), 101, 102, 105
Civil Rights Act (1991, U.S.), 102
civil suits, 45, 51, 84–85, 108, 113
Clinton, Pres. Bill, 38(n9), 49, 50, 81, 124(n7)
Coalition Against Hate Crimes (U.S.), 50(n27)
Commission on Violence Against Women (Sweden), 57–58, 65(n11), 74–75, 77(n22)
Committee on Sexual Crimes (Sweden), 51, 71–72, 88
Commonwealth v. Williams, 79(n26)
Communist Party (now Left Party, Sweden), 29(n14), 53, 89
Community Action Strategies to Stop Rape (CASSR, Ohio), 97(n10)
Comprehensive Employment and Training Act (CETA, U.S.), 41
consciousness-raising, see Sweden, consciousness-raising groups;

Swedish readers will note that the alphabetization has been Anglicized.

United States, consciousness-raising groups
conservative government (Sweden), 54(n33), 55, 74, 107
Copeland, Lois, 38(n8)
corporatism, *see* Sweden, corporatist structure
corroboration requirements, 80, 81, 84, 86, 87, 91
Court of Appeals (U.S.), 101
Crime Bill (1994, U.S.), 50, 81, 83(n30); *see also* Violence Against Women Act (VAWA, U.S.)
criminal justice, *see* Sweden, criminal justice system; United States, criminal justice system

Dahlberg, Anita, 90
DeCrow, Karen, 98
Democratic Party (U.S.), *see* United States, political parties
Department of Labor (U.S.), 41(n13)
Douglass, Frederick, 19(n3)

economic considerations behind progressive policies, vii, 7–11, 31, 94–95
educational institutions, sexual harassment and, 102–103, 106, 108(n21), 113
Environmental Protection Agency (U.S.), 101
Equal Employment Opportunity Commission (EEOC, U.S.), 101–102, 104
Equal Opportunities Act (Act on Equality Between Women and Men at Work; Sweden), 117(n4), 118, 119; concerning sexual harassment, 108, 111–113; government's assessment of, 109(n23), 110; history of, 105, 106, 107
Equal Opportunities Commission, 107(n19)
Equality Ombudsman's Office (JÄMO), 106–107, 108–109, 110, 112, 113, 117, 119
ethnicity, *see* race and racism

family planning policies, 9
Federal Bureau of Investigation (FBI, U.S.), 34, 65
federalism, *see* United States, federalist structure
femicide, 34, 35(n4), 57(n39), 62
feminist, clarified, viii(n4); *see also* Sweden, feminist movement; United States, feminist movement
feminist movement, defined, 8(n9)
foreigners, 115 (n1), 122, 123; *see also* immigrants; xenophobia
Forsberg, Ulla Britt, 41
Forslund, Per-Olov, 73(n18)
Fourteenth Amendment (U.S.), 45, 83
Franklin v. Gwinnett County Public Schools, 103
Frederika Bremer Association (Sweden), 17, 39
FRID-A Projekt (Sweden), 108–109, 111

Geijer, Lennart, 71, 72
gender, clarified, 11–12 (n14); *see also* analysis, gender-specific
Granö, Maria, 72

Hale, Sir Matthew, 80, 82, 86
Harris v. Forklift Systems Inc., 102
Hedlund, Eva, 72, 75
Hill, Anita, 103
Högsta Domstolen, *see* Supreme Court (Sweden)

Illinois Domestic Violence Law, 46(n20)
immigrants 9, 22; *see also* foreigners; xenophobia
incest, 64, 71

job training, 7, 36, 41(n13), 95, 96, 109, 113
journalists, *see* media
judges, *see* Sweden, judges; United States, judges

Kram, Ebon, 42, 117(n4)

labor policies, *see* economic considerations behind progressive policies
labor unions, 4, 7, 105(n17), 106–107, 112–113, 118
Law Enforcement Assistance Administration (LEAA, U.S.), 68
Left Party (Sweden), *see* Communist Party (Sweden)
Legal Aid Committee (Sweden), 89
legislation, 26–27; *see also* Sweden, criminal justice system; United States, criminal justice system
Leijon, Anna-Greta, 53
Levander, Sten, 76
Liberal Party (Sweden), 52, 88
Locke, John, 22
Lutheran Church, 26

magazines, *see* media
Maine Supreme Judicial Court, 79(n26)
Malmö case (Sweden), 87
Mathias, Sen. Charles, 68
media, 117, 122–123; rape and, 71(n14), 73, 75, 80; sexual harassment and, 98, 103(n15), 105(n16); woman battery and, 36
men as perpetrators (generally), 12, 56–57(n38), 116
men's centers (Sweden), 42, 76
Merit Systems Protection Board (MSPB), 99
Meritor Savings Bank v. Vinson, 102
methodology, ix–x, 15
Moderate Party (Sweden), 53, 88
Mott, Lucretia, 19
Ms., *see* media

National American Woman's Suffrage Association, 19, 20
National Association for Sex Education (RFSU, Sweden), 72, 73, 117
National Association of Working Women (U.S.), 94(n3)
National Center for the Prevention of Rape (U.S.), 68

National Clearinghouse on Marital and Date Rape, 82, 83
National Coalition Against Domestic Violence (NCADV, U.S.), 25, 36(n6), 37(n7), 50(n27)
National Council for Crime Prevention (BRÅ, Sweden), 42, 74, 75
National Hate Crimes Statistics Act (U.S.), 50, 51
National Institute for Mental Health (U.S.), 97(n10)
National Institute of Justice (U.S.), 47
National Organization for Women (NOW, U.S.), rape and, 67, 68; sexual harassment and, 98, 112; woman battery and, 35–36, 50(n27)
National Organization of Emergency Shelters for Battered Women (ROKS, Sweden), 39, 42, 55(n37), 56, 59, 117–118
National Rape Prevention Month (U.S.), 80
National Women's Political Caucus (U.S.), 122
New York City Human Rights Commission, 98
New York Radical Feminists (NYRF), 66, 80
newspapers, *see* media
9 to 5 (U.S.), 25
Nineteenth Amendment (U.S.), 20
Norton, Eleanor Holmes, 98

Occupational Safety and Health Act (Sweden), 111
occupational segregation, 14, 95, 109, 113, 114
occupational training, *see* job training
official investigatory reports (SOU, Sweden), 27
ombudsman, 28, *see also* Equality Ombudsman's Office (JÄMO)
Önfelt, Cecilia, 105(n16)
orders of protection (protection orders), 46, 53–55, 59

participant observation, ix
patriarchy, 1, 10, 36, 115, 116, 123
Person, Leif, 71(n14)

Phillips, Wendell, 19
pluralism, 28, 93, 121
Pogrebin, Letty, 105(n16)
police, *see* Sweden, police; United States, police
political culture, *see* Sweden, political culture; United States, political culture
political parties, *see* names of specific Swedish parties; Sweden, political parties; United States, political parties
pornography, 25, 64, 122
professionalization of services, *see* volunteerism and professionalization
prosecutors, *see* Sweden, prosecutors; United States, prosecutors
prostitution, 57(n39), 64(n10), 88, 122
protection orders, *see* orders of protection

Qwist, Gunilla, 88

race and racism, 11, 22(n8), 32(n17), 62, 69, 99(n11), 104; *see also* United States, feminist movement, anti-slavery movement and; xenophobia
rape, 12–15, 61–65; defined, 61(n1); marital and date, 62–63, 82–84, 86, 90–91, 118; Rape Crisis Center (Washington, D.C.), 66; rapist as "victim," 75–76; shield laws, 81; *see also* Sweden, rape; United States, rape
rape crisis centers, *see* Sweden, rape, crisis centers/clinics; Sweden, rape, shelters and; United States, rape, crisis centers/clinics
Reagan, Pres. Ronald, 41(n13), 50
remiss, 27
Republican Party (U.S.), *see* United States, political parties
RFSU, *see* National Association for Sex Education (Sweden)
Rideout, Greta, 82
Röger, Märit, 57, 58–59

ROKS, *see* National Organization of Emergency Shelters for Battered Women (Sweden)
Romanus, Sven, 72

Scott v. Hart, 45
Seneca Falls (New York) convention, 19
sexual abuse of children, 61, 71, 72
sexual harassment (in workplace), 12–15, 94–97; defined, 94(n2); *see also* Sweden, sexual harassment; United States, sexual harassment
sexualized oppression, defined, 56–57
shelters, *see* Sweden, woman battery, shelters; United States, woman battery, shelters
Sheppard-Towner Act (U.S.), 10(n11)
Social Democratic Party (Sweden), 8(n9), 94(n1), 117(n4); Equal Opportunities Act and, 106, 118; rape and, 71, 72(n16), 73–74, 88; sexual harassment and, 107; woman battery and, 40, 53, 56, 57, 59
social policy, defined, vii(n1)
SOU, *see* Official investigatory reports (Sweden)
Stanton, Elizabeth Cady, 19
state structure, 1–3, 115, 123–124; *see also* Sweden, corporatist structure; United States, federalist structure
State v. Oliver, 43
State v. Reed, 79(n26)
statistical data, concerns about, vii–ix; rape and, 62–63, 64–65, 73–74, 77; sexual harassment and, 108, 113; woman battery and, 34, 58
Statistics Bureau (Sweden), *see* Bureau of Statistics (Sweden)
suffrage movement, *see* Sweden, corporatist structure, and suffrage movement; Sweden, feminist movement, history of; United States, federalist structure, and suffrage movement; United States, feminist movement, history of

Superior Court (Pennsylvania), 79(n26)
Supreme Court (Högsta Domstolen, Sweden), 79
Supreme Court (U.S.), 21, 45, 102, 103, 124(n7)
Sweden
  consciousness-raising groups, 25, 39, 109
  corporatist structure, 26–28; and rape, 92, 94; and sexual harassment, 105, 106, 107, 108, 110, 114; and suffrage movement, 16, 20; and woman battery, 33, 36, 51–60, 94; influence on gender-related reform (general), x–xi, 4–5, 7–11, 29–32, 115–119, 123–124
  criminal justice system, 43–44; rape and, 77–79, 86–91; sexual harassment and, 110–112; woman battery and, 51–60
  feminist movement, 8, 25, 118–119, 120; history of, 16–18; hostility to 30–31, 117; rape and, 71, 92; sexual harassment and, 105, 109, 112; woman battery and, 39–40, 59–60
  judges
    rape and, 79; woman battery and, 44
  police
    rape and, 62, 78; woman battery and, 53, 54, 55(n37)
  political culture, 28–32, 116–117; rape and, 71; sexual harassment and, 105; woman battery and, 33, 36, 59–60
  political parties, 117, 118, 120; rape and, 89, 92; sexual harassment and, 106–107; women's sections of, 29, 53, 54, 59, 87, 88, 92, 105; *see also* names of specific parties
  prosecutors
    rape and, 78, 87, 88, 89; sexual harassment and, 108;
  woman battery and, 43, 52, 54, 55
  rape, xi, 53, 62–63, 71–77, 118; criminal justice system and, 77–79, 86–93; crisis centers/clinics, 72, 73, 74, 76, 92, 117, 122–123; sexual harassment and, 107–108; shelters and, 89
  reputation, vii, 7–8, 115–119, 121–122
  sexual harassment, xi, 94–97, 105–114
  woman battery, xi, 33–35, 39–42, 43–44, 73, 74, 118; author's survey of battered women, x, 63; criminal justice system and, 43–44, 51–60, 72–73, 118; shelters, 35, 39–42, 53
Swedish Information Service, 123; *see also* Swedish Institute
Swedish Institute, ix(n5)

Take Back the Night marches, 69
Task Force on Crime (U.S.), 33–34
Task Force on Family Violence (U.S.), 47
temperance, 14(n17)
Thomas, Clarence, 103
Thoreau, Henry David, 22
Thurman, Tracey, 46
Title VII (of Civil Rights Act, U.S.), 101, 105
Title IX (of Civil Rights Act, U.S.), 102–103, 106

unions, *see* labor unions
United States:
  consciousness-raising groups, 24–25; rape and, 66; sexual harassment and, 97; woman battery and, 35
  criminal justice system, 43–51, 119–121; rape and, 68, 77–86; sexual harassment and, 99–105; woman battery and, 43–51
  federalist structure, 20–21; and rape, 92–93; and reform (general), x–xi, 5–7, 16, 20,

24–25, 31–32, 115–116, 119–121, 123–124; and sexual harassment, 104; and suffrage movement, 20, 31; and woman battery, 33, 36, 59–60
feminist movement, 8, 16, 24–25, 119–121; anti-slavery movement and, 18–19; history of, 18–20; rape and, 65, 67, 92; sexual harassment and, 97, 98, 104–105, 108–109
judges
  rape and, 78, 80, 86; woman battery and, 43, 46, 47, 48, 49
police
  rape and, 62, 68, 69, 70, 78, 80, 81–82, 85, 86; woman battery and, 45–49
political culture, 21–25, 31–32; and rape, 82–93; and sexual harassment, 104; and woman battery, 33, 36, 59–60
political parties, 119–120, 122
prosecutors
  rape and, 68, 78; sexual harassment, 108; woman battery, 43, 47, 48
rape, xi, 62–63, 65–70, 76–77; criminal justice system and, 77–86, 91–93, 100; crisis centers/clinics, 66–70
reputation, vii, 7–8, 115–116, 121–122
sexual harassment, xi, 94–105, 108, 109–110, 112–114
woman battery, xi, 33–39, 43–44; rape and, 79; reform of criminal justice system and, 43–44, 59–60; shelters, 35–39

Uppsala University Hospital, 76, 123(n6)

victim-assistance programs, 48, 52, 53, 89
Violence Against Women Act (VAWA, U.S.), 50, 51, 60; *see also* Crime Bill
volunteerism and professionalization, 120; rape and, 66, 67, 68–70, 72, 76, 89, 92; woman battery and, 41–42

Wadstein, Margareta, 106
Wallström, Margot, 56
Westerberg, Bengt, 74
Wilson, Sen. Bob, 82
Wistrand, Birgitta, 39
woman battery, 12–15, 33–35; and rape, 61, 62–63; *see also* Sweden, woman battery; United States, woman battery
Women Against Pornography (U.S.), 25
Women Against Rape groups (U.S.), 67
women as mothers, 7–11, 31, 32
women as workers, 7–11, 31, 32
women's sections, political parties, *see* Sweden, political parties
Working Women United (WWU, U.S.), 98, 100, 112
workplace, sexual harassment in, *see* sexual harassment (in workplace)
World Anti-Slavery Convention, 19

xenophobia, 75, 76, 92, 118

AUTHORS

A Southern Women's Writing Collective, 63(n7)
Adams, Carolyn Teich, 7–8, 17, 24, 25, 59
Allardt, Erik, 26, 28
Anton, Thomas, 28
Bergman, Bo, 33–34(n1)
Bienen, Leigh, 77
Boëthius, Maria-Pia, 61, 71(n14), 76, 87
Butler, Twiss, vii(n2)
Collins, Patricia Hill, 62, 69(n13)
Coontz, Stephanie, 22
Crenshaw, Kimberlè Williams, 11
Dahl, Hans Frederik, 28
Dahlberg, Anita, 3(n4)
Dahlerup, Drude, 1(n1)
Daun, Åke, 28
Davis, Angela, 69(n13)
Dinnerstein, Leonard, 22(n8)
Dobash, R. Emerson, ix
Dobash, Russell, ix
DuBois, Ellen Carol, 17
Eduards, Maud, 29, 105
Enzenberger, Hans Magnus, 30(n15)
Eriksen, Kristin, 33(n1)
Estrich, Susan, 84
Farley, Lin, 97, 98, 100
Foucault, Michel, 64
Freud, Sigmund, 80
Frye, Marilyn, 12
Geis, Gilbert, 77(n23), 90
Gelb, Joyce, 7(n7)
Giddings, Paula, 19
Gordon, Linda, 1(n1)
Grimstad, Kristen, 67(n12)
Haavio-Mannila, Elina, 17, 31
Hagman, Ninni, 112
Heclo, Hugh, 23, 29, 30, 115(n1)
Hernes, Gudmund, 4(n5)
Hernes, Helga, 30
Hirshman, Linda, 51
Hydén, Margareta, 33–34(n1)
Jonung, Christina, 9
Kelman, Steven, 23(n9)
Krasner, Steven, 6
Langelan, Martha J., 96, 97(n9, n10), 99(n11)
Leghorn, Lisa, 9, 10
Lerman, Lisa G., 48(n24)
Lindau, Rebecka, 117(n2)
Lipset, Seymour Martin, 21
Lundgren, Eva, 33–34(n1), 55–56
MacKinnon, Catherine A., 11(n14), 61, 63, 64(n8), 84, 101
Madsen, Henrik, 23, 29, 30, 115(n1)
Martin, Del, 35(n5)
McCombs, Annie, 32(n17)
Morrison, Toni, 103(n15)
Norris, Pippa, 8
Parker, Katherine, 9, 10
Pateman, Carole, 1(n3), 9(n10)
Pendo, Elizabeth, 50(n27)
Peterson, Eric, 27
Pleck, Elizabeth, 3(n4), 14(n17)
Rennie, Susan, 67(n12)
Rhode, Deborah, 79, 103
Rich, Adrienne, 123
Ruggie, Mary, 8, 9
Ruin, Olof, 58
Russell, Diana E. H., 62, 63, 82
Sainsbury, Diane, 6
Sapiro, Virginia, 10
Sassoon, Anne Showstack, 1(n1)
Schecter, Susan, 37
Schirmer, Jennifer, 9
Scott, Hilda, 30
Selvik, Arne, 4(n5)
Skard, Torild, 17, 31
Stanley, Liz, ix(n6)
Thordarsson, Bodil, 9
Tiby, Eva, 27(n12)
Tilly, Charles, 12
Vinciguerra, Marlisa, 100(n13)
Walby, Sylvia, 1(n1)
Warrior, Betsy, 36
Weber, Max, 1, 10
Williams, Patricia, 37, 44(n17)
Wilson, Elizabeth, 1(n1)
Winston, Kathryn Teich, 8, 17, 24, 25, 59
Wise, Sue, ix(n6)
Woolf, Virginia, 1

www.ingramcontent.com/pod-product-compliance
Lightning Source LLC
Chambersburg PA
CBHW071207070526
44584CB00019B/2948